BING CROSBY

BING CROSBY

Michael Freedland

ISIS
LARGE PRINT
Oxford and Orlando

First published in Great Britain 1998
by Chameleon Books, an imprint of André Deutsch Ltd

Published in Large Print 1999 by ISIS Publishing Ltd,
7 Centremead, Osney Mead, Oxford OX2 0ES,
ISIS Publishing, PO Box 195758, Winter Springs,
Florida 32719-5758
by arrangement with André Deutsch

British Library Cataloguing in Publication Data
Freedland, Michael
  Bing Crosby. – Large print ed.
  1. Crosby, Bing 2. Motion picture actors and actresses –
  United States – Biography 3. Singers – United States –
  Biography 4. Large type books
  I. Title
  782.4'2'164'092

      ISBN 0-7531-5099-9

Printed and bound by MPG Books Ltd, Bodmin, Cornwall

CONTENTS

CHAPTER ONE

Bingo

History has a place for Bing Crosby, owner of a strange name, possessed of a unique voice, a man whose style was as unorthodox as his dress sense. His penchant for ill-matching socks and loud check shirts was his trademark of sorts, but his voice was naturally unmistakable. Many other singers who came along at the time of his greatest triumph tried to copy him, but never succeeded.

So was that all there was? The voice undoubtedly had a magical quality about it, but there was more to the youngster christened Harry Lillis Crosby than that — his iconic status did not come cheaply. The Academy of Motion Picture Arts and Sciences paid respect to his multiple talents when they gave him an Oscar. More significantly, perhaps, he was hugely popular with his audience. For years, he topped all the polls.

This man with hair so thin he tried to wear a hat even in bedroom scenes, and with protruding ears that were beyond sticking back, women found so attractive that they sent him letters offering all kinds of services not specified in the Actors Equity rule book. This man was a powerful comedian who had serious views on many things — business, making money, and, most serious of all, a sense of discipline for his sons that could have earned him employment as a nineteenth-century workhouse master.

But most of all he was that singer. His frequent sparring partner, Bob Hope, would say that Crosby had the greatest voice of all time. Now, that is saying something, but it isn't quite true. There were better popular singers, vocalists who worked and projected voices that could shake a Broadway theatre without the help of a microphone. And certainly few opera buffs would agree with the man with the ski-slope nose. But you have to say that in a world where style was ever-important, he had it in spades.

For forty years, from the time when Jolson gave up his throne as king of show business to the era when Sinatra was incontestably the monarch, Bing Crosby was popular music. Certainly, he was the most important crooner of his time. Which leads us to pose the question — are crooners worthy of serious attention?

In our history, undoubtedly. If for only for this reason: at fashionable dances, at church socials, in youth clubs, for a certain period, every male who ever got up before a microphone fancied himself as a crooner and, consciously or unconsciously, was imitating Bing Crosby.

Even more significantly, he revolutionized home entertainment — simply by being single-handedly responsible for killing off the parlour piano. Those fans who resent that suggestion should consider what Crosby achieved. If Al Jolson was the first pop star, Crosby was the very first to turn pop singing into big business. The people who loved him helped him create and nurture that very business. Year after year, week in week out, there was a new Bing Crosby record. More than 400,000 were sold in his lifetime. At one time in the late 1940s and early 1950s, there was almost no song that Bing didn't sing — the sort of verse that helped him make his fortune.

From his theme song "Where The Blue Of The Night Meets The Gold Of The Day", through "Please", to "Dear Hearts And Gentle People" and, of course "White Christmas", Bing Crosby sang them all. Hits from other people's movies, songs that competitors introduced in their radio shows, the chart-toppers of their day (not that the phrase was current then), the big songs from the big shows, Bing sang them all. And on the way, a massive collection of those Crosby's Own tunes, numbers that would for ever be identified with him. These were standard songs which he turned into song standards, which is not at all the same thing.

He would dismiss it all modestly. "My notion of singing was to make a sound which resembled the human voice with a bubble in it." That was a fair assessment of the way it sounded. But what a human voice! What a bubble!

It's hard to analyse Bing Crosby. It's harder still to pinpoint what made the man with the easy-going voice unique. But then maybe that's just what it was — an easy-going voice. He'd always had that. It went with his easy-going personality. Boys and girls who went to school with him at Spokane in Washington State testified to that for years.

Since then, however, it has become fashionable to tell a different Crosby story, depicting him as a vicious, unfeeling abuser of his children; a martinet, a drunk, a bully. None of that fits with the image that made Crosby the outstanding entertainer of his day — in fact, of so many days, so many years, so many generations that it is difficult to pinpoint his own actual era.

Perhaps, if you could describe him as simply "Crosby, that well-known star of the 1930s", it would be easier to pigeon-hole him. You could say that success had come early, that there were always a great number of hangers-on, that he was insecure, unsure that his voice would last, and embarrassed by the fact that a green light looked red to him and that he could never be sure which pair of socks to wear. Also that in the 1940s he was the biggest thing around and that, well into the 1950s, they didn't come much bigger. Ten years later, he was still making records and, just before he died in the 1970s, was topping the bill at the London Palladium, the temple of international variety.

The man who sold more records than any human being ever before had a voice like no other. Yet he would never recognize it as anything special — until he worked out how much money and fame it brought him, that is. Indeed, it was, at first hearing, quite an ordinary voice. Listen to it just once and he sounded like every other popular singer — or crooner. He wasn't a Caruso or an early incarnation of a Pavarotti. His voice didn't have the resonance of his own first idol, Al Jolson, none of the vocal twists and twirls, the acrobatics that made Jolson so famous. He didn't have the style of Sinatra, who always sounded as though he worked on a lyric much as a concert pianist practised a concerto — every sound, every line, every verse, every phrase perfectly crafted. Crosby wasn't like that. He was . . . well, easy-going.

He sang the way it came out whenever he opened his mouth. Ask him if he were a tenor or a baritone, he would never have known — until critics started telling him. He was a baritone, with a gift to make a simple song sound as though it were recorded through pure silk.

He discovered that gift very early in Spokane, the fourth of the seven children of Harry Lowe Crosby and his wife Katherine. The family remembered him singing from almost the moment he stopped crying.

That was in Tacoma, Washington, a little place about as far west as you can get in America before falling into the Pacific Ocean. But it wasn't part of the glamorous West Coast which he would one day dominate. This was in the far north-west, where it gets cold in winter, very cold indeed — the sort of place where White Christmases were not just dreamed about, but were part of life. Maybe that accounts in part for Crosby's success: when he sang that most successful of all popular tunes — and let no one say that Elton John's tribute to Princess Diana, "Candle In The Wind", has eclipsed it — he had lived it and it came from the heart.

The folk of Spokane, where Harry Lillis Crosby went to school and grew up, also expected people to do things from the heart. Katherine, who had been brought up in the Catholic Church, expected her fourth son to be a priest. The nearest he got to that was to look as if the dog collar had been grafted on to his neck when he took "holy orders" in two hugely popular films, *Going My Way* and *The Bells Of St. Mary's*.

Other actors had played priests in the movies before and would do so after him — at one time it was the most popular profession in the movies. But Spencer Tracy, Pat O'Brien, Humphrey Bogart and even Frank Sinatra would have had to have doffed those soft, black ecclesiastical fedoras and agree that Crosby was the best priest Hollywood ever had. Somehow you knew that he was receiving inspiration from the men of the cloth back in his childhood.

He didn't stay Harry Crosby for long. That name was always his father's. Harry, it was said, came from Viking stock, and indeed the name Crosby was Danish — it means "Town of the Cross", which complements nicely the religious upbringing for the children who bore that name. But it was Irish Catholicism, as practiced by the Tacoma priests, that ruled in the Crosby household.

Harry was by all accounts a pleasant man. Not successful, just a book-keeper. But he was spoken of with the kind of respect most fathers would hope to achieve. Whether that respect went along with love is not apparent. There appears to have been a certain estrangement in later years, but the reasons are not clear. The feelings the children all had for Katherine Crosby were more easily definable.

She was a Harrigan, which was as Irish as it sounds and accounts for the fact that her brother George, young

Harry's favourite uncle, sang George M. Cohan's song "Harrigan" whenever there was a piano ready to have a few chords struck and a glass of Irish whiskey to go with it.

They weren't an immigrant family, at least not the kind that so many American entertainers would boast. Both sets of Crosby grandparents had gone to Canada and it was there that Katherine and Harry were born. They crossed the border into the United States because they hoped it would bring the kind of prosperity that had eluded them.

Harry Lillis Crosby was born in 1903 — not 1904, as appears in many of the official Crosby records, nor the 1901 that is sometimes claimed (and which appeared on some biographical matter he approved himself). Baptism records confirm the date as 1903.

How Harry Lillis became Bing has never been the subject of controversy, although differing theories have been advanced. It was an age when "yellow journalism" brought comic strips into homes all over America. Children were introduced to newspapers via those strips, which had as big a following among youngsters as television does today. They were grabbed by kids the moment the papers were thrown on to front lawns or left in mail boxes outside apartment buildings. The strip that young Harry devoured was called "The Bingsville Bugle". Its main character was Bingo. Harry's young friend Valentine Hobart loved the comic, too, but not with the same fascination as young Harry — he was addicted to it. So Valentine began calling Harry "Bingo". The name caught on, and other people soon started dropping the "o". Another story says that he liked playing with a toy gun and used to run around his house, shouting "Bing-bing-bing". As he once wrote, his memory was "like an out-of-kilter juke box. When I drop a nickel into it, I am not sure which story it will play back."

One fact we can be sure of is that, before long, Harry was the name reserved for the father of the clan. Like Pip in *Great Expectations*, as far as the junior Harry was concerned, Bing he became and Bing he remained. For ever afterwards. It could be argued that without such a name to set him apart, Bing Crosby might never have made it as big as he did — and big is an understatement. But the name was just one fairly insignificant part of a multi-faceted character: not just a singer, but a comic, and sometimes a serious, actor worthy of the Oscar he won. (This tribute was bestowed to the not-inconsiderable chagrin of that other name-changer, Crosby's frequent movie partner, Bob Hope. Leslie Townes Hope had felt, with a fair amount of certainty, that his parents' choice would need altering if it was to go up in lights.)

Of course, looking back on it all now, it is easy to imagine that young Master Crosby fitted the name so perfectly simply because he looked like a Bing — or rather a Bingo, a character with big floppy ears. Bing's own ears were as protruding and as essential a part in his appearance as the hat he wore and the pipe he smoked.

They joked about those ears in Spokane and in Hollywood, too. He would agree at first to having them stuck down, but later balked at the notion almost just as he would complain about having to wear a toupee. But in Spokane, he was just one of the boys and would deal with the kids who taunted him over his ears in the same way that he dealt with those who laughed at the somewhat excessive weight of his sister Mary Rose.

Those who witnessed his approach to these matters wondered if he would become a boxer. As it was, he started singing at school and in church and for seventy-odd years citizens of the town who would boast that they predicted the seven-year-old boy would one day be a great singer.

Life in Spokane was like that in many another smallish American town where everyone knew everyone else. But it wasn't one of those sleepy, homespun places so beloved of early Hollywood movies (the kind where the young men wore striped blazers and the librarian was too sassy for her own good). It was a busy place and nice Catholic people like the Crosbys were taught to be busy, too — just so long as they left time for going to church, learning the catechism and raising their hats when the priest walked past.

Respect and hard work — that was how it was for families like theirs. Mom and Pop Crosby and Bing's elder brothers, Larry and Everett, who would play significant roles as their younger brother's career developed. Indeed, the baby of the family, who became known as Bob, would make his own mark in show business. In fact, if his brother hadn't turned out to be such a powerhouse of a performer, Bob Crosby, band-leader and head of the group known as The

Bobcats, would have been the big star not just in the Crosby brood but in the whole of Spokane, too.

As things turned out, Bing Crosby was before long to be the city's favourite son. And even today, more than two decades after his death, they still talk of him with the kind of pride they would have felt had Abraham Lincoln been born there rather than in his log cabin in Illinois. You might still find a few extremely old men and women in Spokane who will remember the Bing Crosby they say they knew at school, and even in his own pensionable years he would speak only affectionately of the place — so very different from a certain Frank Sinatra, who showed nothing but contempt for his own home town of Hoboken, New Jersey.

No. Crosby always talked of Spokane as the important place in his life — and spoke as though he meant it. He was educated there, firstly at the Webster Grade School, then later at Gonzaga High School and finally the town's college. The Jesuits at Gonzaga would have liked to think that a life based on good thoughts and homage to the Virgin Mary would be enough for any man.

The boy whose mother wanted him to be a priest had to satisfy himself — and her — with the role of altar boy. As for many another youngster who walked in line, dressed in a crisp white surplice, behind the priest, there was in those incense-filled surroundings a mixture of spirituality and theatre. What he may not have got from the first, he compensated with the second.

It would all be good training for the man who one day would specialize in heartfelt entertaining. But whether it would be good for the family he had later in life one can't now be sure — for there was an additional feature to it all. The church instilled a sense of discipline that he expected from other people — if not always from himself.

In fact, in those days, there was little that was disciplined about him. To his teachers he was noticeably lazy, which went against the grain in a Jesuit institution. He liked sports — which was a certain compensation in the world of Pat O'Brien-like ball-playing Fathers — but wasn't terribly good at them. He would have liked to have been a successful basketball player, but every time he jumped it was as though those flapping ears turned into wings and made him take off in the wrong direction. Swimming was a different matter. He loved the water and the water loved him, helped no doubt by the blubber that even as a youngster he was developing.

Anyone listening to the adult Bing Crosby had to be struck by his use of language. It was at Gonzaga that he first began to realize the importance of being articulate, of expressing oneself in a varied and creative manner. Hence later there were laughs to be had from introducing guest artists on his radio shows with an assembly of statements that would have done credit to the chairman at an old-time British music hall. Of course, he did overdo it, but being able to twist his tongue assuredly through convoluted monologues proved to be a fine complement to the more familiar elements of his show.

Indeed, he used it to good account while at Gonzaga. He was very active in the debating society. So active that he was the one they looked to when the more scholarly section of the student body thought it necessary to discuss the vital issues of the day. He formed a group that set itself up to destroy whatever arguments about whatever subject the "Establishment" chose to raise. It was a time when the Russian Revolution was still fresh in people's minds and the inconvenient details of Stalinism hadn't yet percolated as far as Washington State. Bing decided to call his group the "Bolsheviks". They had no idea what the word meant. Two generations later when Senator McCarthy was hunting for reds under all the Hollywood beds, Bing chose to forget the name altogether.

But he never forgot Gonzaga. He never tried to suggest that he was a product of some Ivy League college. If, when he was a superstar, they asked him to help them raise money for the college, he was always ready to oblige, a gesture he was not ready to extend to other charities.

Nevertheless, if he did always retain that special affection for his school, there was another institution in the town which provided the most influential aspect of his education — although for a time he might have wondered if he was going to be struck down by a fork of lightning. For him, the Auditorium Theatre was something akin to a temple. Seeing the great acts perform there was almost a religious experience.

At the Auditorium he heard Al Jolson and watched mesmerized as he performed black-faced in shows like *Robinson Crusoe Jnr*. "He was the first big influence in my life," Crosby was to tell me some twenty-five years ago. "He was like a whirlwind." It was perhaps the first indication of where the youngster everyone called Bing was heading.

Jolson convinced him that he wanted to spend his own life singing on that big beautiful stage. He played the drums in a band at the university called The Juicy Seven, using the school's instruments. But it wasn't going to make him any money. At 19 his family was breathing down his neck and it was time to think about a career. Bing decided to become a lawyer. It was not a good decision. Bored out of his mind, he studied law at Gonzaga in the morning and worked in the offices of Mr Charles S. Albert in the afternoon. Something had to give and luckily, sitting nearby in the Auditorium, equally mesmerised, had been another young citizen of Spokane by the name of Al — Al Rinker. They decided to do something about their shared ambition: they would both go into show business — together.

CHAPTER TWO

Two Boys And A Piano

It was the perfect example of being in the right place with the right person at the right time. If any Crosby student wants to know how it all began, the single moment that set Bing on the path to show business stardom has to be when he and Al Rinker slapped each other around the shoulder and decided they had a lot in common. Not that the future was anything like assured. Few now recall the fact, but there was a time when it looked as though Bing Crosby would be remembered, if at all, as a drummer. For that was how he appeared on a stage for the first time — and got money for it.

He had been a percussionist at school dances. Now, though, school and college were in the past, both for Bing and for his pal Al Rinker. Rinker wasn't the easy-going languid type that Bing was. While Crosby was seemingly content to let life happen to him whichever way it chose, Rinker was more intent on shaping his own destiny and was focused on making music. He had his own "group" (as, of course, it was *not* known in those days). He called them the Musicaladers. Would Bing Crosby like to be a Musicalader? It was an invitation he could not refuse.

One of the reasons he couldn't refuse was because he admired Rinker and the seriousness with which he took his work. After all, this was a man with a musical pedigree. His sister, Mildred Bailey, was already earning herself a reputation as one of the best female jazz singers in the country — and one of the very few white women in what was largely regarded as a black person's art.

Right from the beginning, Bing enjoyed being on any of the few bandstands which granted the Musicaladers the opportunity to perform. He particularly enjoyed the cheque he received after each dance — a generous sum totalling no less than $5.

What he especially enjoyed, apart from the chance to pound his own set of drums — bearing a big sunset on the bass drum — was to get up in the middle of a number and pick up a megaphone. Dance band singers all over America used them to project their voices in those pre-microphone years. The sight — and the sound — of the megaphone-bearing singers accompanying those sweat-drenched masochists taking part in marathon dance contests is a definitive image of the 1920s. Rudy Vallee, whom some people consider to have been the world's first crooner — although Bing's later rival Russ Colombo would be a competitor for the title — adopted the horn as his trademark.

Now Bing Crosby picked up the instrument to join in as the band played "For Me And My Gal" and "Hindustan". But it wasn't just the usual stuff of the age that they played. As he would later write, the choices were always "ragged but novel". He explained: "The other musicians could read notes, but they could not play

15

stuff the way we played it. Young folks liked us and two or three nights a week we got dates to play at high school dances and private parties. We pulled down three dollars apiece for a night's work."

It was a high voice, a pure one, too, with no suggestion of the "boo-boo-be-boos" that would later be so closely identified with the "Old Groaner". But then The Groaner was still very young, barely 20 years old.

He liked to sing and before long it became very clear that the dancers liked to hear him. In fact, it didn't require a very close look to realize that they liked his vocalizing a great deal more than they liked his drumming. In a matter of weeks, the Musicaladers had broken up, the drums were put away, the band was made smaller and Messrs Crosby and Rinker were a team. Just who was going to be the real star was a matter of speculation.

These were exciting times in American show business. As far as singers and popular musicians were concerned, vaudeville was still big business, the one they all wanted to break into first. The big time would come later. The first night that Bing himself stood on a stage and performed with a real orchestra would be at the city's Clemmer Theatre, which was about as big as things got in those parts.

He and Al liked the pose of being the gay young blades about town, as they might have put it back in the 1920s. They were as distinctly heterosexual as they were keen to break the Prohibition laws. Bing Crosby and alcohol were becoming a potent mix. Give the young man a girl on his arm — or sitting on his lap, a very daring thing to do seventy-odd years back — and a cup of bathtub hooch and he was a happy fellow.

And why not? Wasn't life there for the enjoying? Certainly, they found little reason not to do so. Singing was fun. Why work at it? In this he was totally different from his idol, Mr Jolson. The man who called himself "The World's Greatest Entertainer", and rarely heard anyone challenge his self-appointed title, toiled at his task of keeping an audience in ecstasies as hard as any labourer breaking stones and building a road.

That was not the Crosby way, not at all the style of the man who was most happy singing while Al Rinker pounded a piano. He sang as though he happened to find a note or two coming to him while he was in the shower, which might be indicative of how he practised. He didn't rehearse. Until managements started asking questions about the size of the repertoire that Bing could boast, he was happy to keep singing the same songs. "Five Feet Two" and "Margie" were the centre-pieces of most performances — during which Bing sometimes felt so languid he would join Al in the orchestra pit to sing from there because he thought it was less of a strain. A strange tendency, considering not just the relationship Bing Crosby would later have with his audiences, but also the huge output Crosby would later produce. Astonishing to even put the words limited repertoire and Bing together.

They were earning something like $30 a week now, but that was to dry up, too. Starting out in show business was not the easiest way of making a living. Al's sister Mildred was singing at a place called the Silver Grill; they decided to pack up Bing's set of drums and whatever they could cram into a couple of suitcases and go to visit her. It wasn't just the idea of the Silver Grill that appealed so much, although it was a plusher establishment than either of the boys had ever known before. It was its location, a little way down the Pacific coast. Actually, it was a thousand miles down the Pacific coast — in Hollywood.

It was a busy, crazy place in those days. Jolson had just made *The Jazz Singer*, the world's first "talkie". So the town was abuzz with speculation about which studio was going to fail and which would come to terms with this revolutionary microphone, which was striking fear into some of the studios.

They travelled to Los Angeles in an old ramshackle Model-T Ford they had bought for $30 — so old and so ramshackle that it didn't even have a roof. Convertibles were not yet a status symbol. In those days, you had either lost the roof or were too poor to buy a car that was covered. Crosby and Rinker were poor, but had probably never been happier.

It wasn't too long before they found work. An impresario called Arthur Freed came to their aid and put them in a vaudeville act. Freed would later, with his partner Will Morrissey, put on shows at LA's Orange Grove called *Morrissey's Music Hall Revue*. He was also the songwriter who created "Singin' In The Rain", "Our Love Is Here To Stay" and "Be A Clown". But more significantly, he would run the outfit that made the famous Gene Kelly musicals — the inspiration behind the fabled "Freed Unit" at MGM. Back then, though, neither Freed nor Crosby were thinking about

Hollywood as the movie town, the place where they would have their triumphs.

It was enough that Bing and Rinker were having fun once more, earning a regular living and drinking more than they should have done. In San Francisco they were in their alcoholic element, finding admission to the neighbourhood speakeasies — once the man behind the spyhole recognized them as unlikely police informers — and drinking pure gin from china cups.

On one occasion, he and Rinker entertained a group of college students at Berkeley University and ended up in a water fountain. A regular assortment of chorus girls in the music hall saw to their other needs.

Ben Lyon — the Hollywood silent star who became famous in Britain during the Second World War and would later be known for discovering a girl called Norma Jean Baker and making her Marilyn Monroe — told me about watching Crosby and Rinker in LA nightspots when they drove the old Model-T down south again. "He kept disappearing. Then I realized he was being held up by someone standing behind him. He was blind drunk. But when he stood up, if not straight, then slightly diagonally, you could just about make out a quite pleasant voice." Not yet a great voice, but then the easy-going Mr Crosby wasn't after stardom. At that stage, he just wanted to make enough to give him a living that he was going to enjoy.

They were billing themselves now as Two Boys And A Piano (Singing Songs Their Own Way). It wasn't very original, but it appealed to the audience at Hollywood's Metropolitan Theatre. By now they were getting $150 a week for an act which brought such applause that the chandeliers at the giant theatre shook — no mean achievement in those days, when amplification was so primitive it hardly picked up a complete sentence, let alone a whole song. It says a great deal for the power of these two youngsters over an audience that it simply didn't matter. They were just beginning in show business, but they had already learned the number-one lesson — put every effort into the job in hand. As we have seen, this was not an easy thing for Bing himself to do. In fact, it was contrary to everything he stood for — when he wasn't being held up from behind, that is. He would soon decide there was an easier way to make a living.

There was one other thing about these two boys and their piano. They sounded new and fresh and, in the midst of these Prohibition days, people were looking for just that. The Metropolitan was owned by the Paramount Publix organization, the outfit which in a few years would become Paramount Pictures. Bing himself couldn't have realized at the time that it was the beginning of a career-long relationship. At that stage of his life, he couldn't think that far ahead — or maybe he didn't want to.

Under contract with Paramount, these two boys and their keyboard commuted between the Metropolitan and the Granada in San Francisco. They still seemed to do it nice and easy, but the customers realized they were getting their money's worth. Rinker had some exciting new arrangements. And then, they flipped a coin — and a pretty valuable coin their $300 a week was in 1926 —

20

they abandoned the sweet just-as-it-comes routine and went crazy, doing a dance act that was deliberately the worst thing seen on either of the two stages; you were either very good to get booked into these theatres or very bad. In the latter case your act was, in the manner of Tommy Cooper, trading on your badness so that the audience lapped it up like a cat with a dish of cream.

At the Metropolitan and the Granada, it was easy to be caught up in the enthusiasm of it all. It was infectious, and to people in the business that was the best thing about it. Surrounded by such huge appreciation, it was difficult not to think you were having a great time, even if your best instincts told you that you didn't like it at all. Among those caught up in the excitement was a man who was always on the look-out for new talent — a manager called Jimmy Gillespie whose hottest property at that point was the band leader, "Pops".

Pops — aka Paul Whiteman — was big. He was a whale of a man whose several chins wobbled when he walked. He bore a passing resemblance to Oliver Hardy, with a similar little black moustache, but next to him Ollie was a midget. Yet it wasn't just his personal bulk that made Pops a national institution. Paul Whiteman was the most popular band leader in America.

On stage, he moved as little as possible — a 300-pound figure like his had to have other qualities and he had them almost to excess. He dressed with as much style and flair as a man a third his size, and his charisma matched his paunch. People queued up for tickets when he was appearing — because they knew they were going to get a great show. He had as much draw as the horseshoe-shaped household magnets of the time. But instead of picking up mother's hairpins, what Whiteman picked us was an enormous following. As Crosby would later say, he was "above other band leaders as Mount Everest stands out above other mountains".

He had been very big — in appeal as well as in appearance — for years now, but his reputation had been greatly enhanced by a concert at New York's Aeolian Hall just a couple of years earlier. That was when he fronted his orchestra for the first performance of a new work, with the composer, George Gershwin, playing the piano solo.

Introducing *Rhapsody In Blue* to an audience made up of a combination of Manhattan's social register and the biggest names in the music business enhanced Whiteman's reputation beyond all expectations. Not only had the young composer Gershwin, hitherto known only as a songwriter, become a respected musical personality, but the conductor had risen to a new level of respectability.

Whiteman was indeed a superstar. The first of the superstar big band leaders. He also had a degree of self-importance which did not make him any less loveable to the people who worked with him. He believed in his right to delegate. His frame was too big, his breath control too limited, to spend his recreation hours in doing more than the eating which was essential to him and his way of life.

That was why Jimmy Gillespie was so important to him. Gillespie was his trusted manager; trusted, that is, to make decisions that Pops would not consider ridiculous. After watching and hearing the Two Boys And A Piano at the Metropolitan he went round to see his boss at the Million Dollar Theatre. "I've seen a couple of boys I think will be just right for us," he said.

Whiteman asked the two to come down to see him at the theatre and spoke to them over glasses of champagne and caviar (at least that was the way Bing reported it — Al Rinker would remember the liquid refreshment as having come from a local brewery). He agreed to hire the duo, sound unheard.

Soon, Crosby and Rinker had severed their relationship with Paramount Publix, and were part of the Paul Whiteman organization. Neither would regret the move, although there would be a few moments when everyone concerned did wonder about the wisdom of the decision.

CHAPTER
THREE

Bad Vibrations

It was a moment of inspiration — for both Bing and Pops Whiteman. Now, all these years later, it is worth asking how different the Crosby career would have been had he not been invited to join what even now is regarded as the best band of its era. What is certain is that neither imagined they were about to launch the career of one of the great solo artists of the 20th century. The fact had to be faced that Bing didn't appear to be star material. Stars were handsome and Bing had that problem with his ears. There was also a hairline that was beginning to recede to the point of oblivion. And then . . . well, any number of attractive young females could testify to the fact that, when they came close to his waistline, it was rather more substantial than the ideal.

But was stardom merely appearance? Not when it came to singers, it wasn't. Over the years, students of the entertainment industry have tried to analyse which qualities determine popularity and success, but these, of course, change over time and vary between art forms. In the late 1920s, it still was either a great lover on screen or a great singer on stage; the kind who opened out his arms, like Jolson, and could positively feel the audience rushing into his embrace, like the crowd at his "home" the Winter Garden. Crosby wasn't that kind of singer at all.

Nor, of course, was Bing used to taking part in that love-fest which a professional popular singer needed. He was merely delighted to sign on the bottom line and take Al Rinker off for a drink while they talked about the next show. Not too long, mind, it took up too much drinking time and occupied minds that were more concentrated on finding a woman.

The Whiteman opportunity wasn't the only one that had come their way, so they were feeling about as contented as only two young men convinced they were on the threshold of great careers can be. In October 1926, at the Biltmore Theatre in Los Angeles, they made a record, a duet called "I've Got The Girl". It wasn't a hit, but it was the very first 78 rpm disc to have the name Bing Crosby on the label — the first of uncountable thousands (considering how many pirate versions have surfaced over the years) by the man who was to revolutionize the art of recording popular songs.

In fact, the engineers thought that Bing was singing the song too slowly — so they speeded it up. It was to be more than seventy years, when a Crosby enthusiast released an original take of the song, before anyone could hear what Bing's performance really sounded like. But even recording it at the right speed wouldn't have made much difference to the flipside, as it would be called a generation or two later; "Idolizing" was pretty terrible.

Now Whiteman promised them more. They recorded "Wistful And Blue" with the band and it caught on with

25

the record-buying public the way the first disc had not. Rinker and Crosby were virtually an overnight sensation, even if it *had* seemed to have been a long night.

The two of them went from venue to venue, city to city, Al playing his piano, Bing singing his songs, none of them too demanding or much worth remembering today. The audiences loved them. Pops clapped his pudgy hands along with the audience and Bing and Al smiled, half wondering what it was that made them so popular.

They simply had the right material for the right time. Crooning was popular and the way Bing did it was different enough to have crowds cheering him every time they appeared at a comfortable small theatre, in any part of the country.

However, there has to be a qualification to that statement — and an underlining of the word "small". Whiteman was well respected wherever he went, and the people who paid a couple of dollars for the best seats in a theatre in Chicago or San Francisco were enthusiastic for everything he offered them. In Peoria or Duluth they were ecstatic. New York had to be the same story, didn't it? Well, actually, it didn't.

The Whiteman orchestra opened at the Paramount Theatre, got all the cheers and claps that they expected and its conductor beamed as he introduced the two boys and their piano. That was when things started to change. You can't see much that is going on from the stage, not with that big spotlight staring you in the face. You can't hear much that is going on at the other side of the footlights. What you *can* detect is what the paying customers are feeling.

On the first, second and third nights at the Paramount, Whiteman felt it — and didn't like what he felt. The vibrations were wrong; the vibrations of people shuffling in their seats. Sometimes it was the sound of them moving into the aisles and walking out. Above all, the electricity just wasn't flowing. When Crosby and Rinker appeared, the current that *had* switched on the audience for the earlier part of the show suddenly failed.

It didn't take long after that for the theatre manager plainly to order Whiteman to leave the two out of the show. There was no proper amplification at the theatre — good microphones were as rare as air conditioning — and people who paid to see a show and risk suffering the stifling heat of summer in New York were not happy to have to strain their ears, too. Besides, who in that sophisticated Manhattan audience wanted to hear this music from the sticks? It was bad enough that the duo had come to New York from California, but to have originally hailed from Spokane? To coin a later Crosby song hit . . . please.

For once, Mr Crosby was concerned about the way his career was going. Whiteman told Bing and his partner not to bother to turn up to do their act. But he had to pay them. There was a contract that said as much. So he found them additional work — like getting Bing to strike the bells for the Paul Whiteman interpretation of the *1812 Overture*. That was a kind of humiliation they didn't subject people to in Spokane. A little better was the opportunity to broadcast — as part of the Whiteman chorus.

Bing told his parents and brothers and sisters to listen to their radio. The Crosby family told their neighbours who, in turn, told all their friends about the local boys who had made good. They switched on. They waited. They listened. Bing's mother was convinced she heard him at one point, but couldn't be sure and the rest of the family simply shrugged their shoulders to humour her. But they stayed tuned and waited for the final announcements. No mention of Bing Crosby. Not a sound to indicate he was part of the operation, let alone that he was one of the members of the chorus.

All three men whose names had been on the Whiteman contract began to doubt the wisdom of taking out their fountain pens. For Pops it was a mistake that he was ready to put down to experience. For Al and Bing it signalled the end of what had looked like being a very exciting career.

It was thanks to a man named Matty Malneck that the words "The End" did not appear on any stories concerning the partnership. Malneck — later to be an honoured name in the history of popular music as the leader of a highly successful orchestra — worked as an arranger for Whiteman before taking out his viola and heading numerous combos of his own. It was he who suggested that the two team up with another pianist for whom he had ambitions, a youngster called Harry Berris.

A trio, he was convinced, had more going for it than any duo. Whiteman, who had two salaries to pay whether Bing and Al worked for him or not, thought it was worth trying. So did Bing and Al. Overnight, the two fellows with their piano had become the Rhythm Boys.

CHAPTER
FOUR

The Rhythm Boys

Sammy Cahn hadn't yet written his big hit, "Call Me Irresponsible", but if he had known Bing Crosby forty years earlier he couldn't have thought of a more appropriate theme. Bing was always the more irresponsible of the two, which might or might not explain why he was the one who became the superstar. In the kindest way, he was the naughty boy. We can argue now that he provided lessons for all the big entertainers who followed in his footsteps, that after meeting Matty Malneck he settled down to the hard grind of making a name for himself. Actually, he didn't. Yes, he did make a name for himself, but it wasn't one he would have wanted engraved on his tombstone. He was as lazy and as fun-loving as any pop star of the 1990s.

Except, of course, he wasn't a pop star yet. Matty Malneck's inspired suggestion of teaming Two Boys And A Piano with Harry Berris deserves to go down into history along with Jolson's black-face, Harpo Marx's silence and four Liverpool lads finding themselves unusual haircuts to augment their unusual name. Not that the Rhythm Boys were the Beatles of their day. Had

Messrs Crosby, Rinker and Berris climbed into a time machine and faced The Beatles in a contest, John, Paul, Ringo and George would have had little to worry about. But the Rhythm Boys had something, nevertheless. And Paul Whiteman was the first to recognize the fact.

Crosby, Rinker and Berris were now Paul Whiteman's Rhythm Boys — the name of Pops *had* to go along as part of the title. But they did sound different, administering harmonics like a Southern preacher warning of evil times ahead. And just as a spell-binding preacher would have congregations enthralled, the Rhythm Boys — sorry, the Paul Whiteman Rhythm Boys — had audiences jumping in their seats.

Bing and Al did much as they had always been doing, while Berris added two important new elements: his deep, powerful voice, which projected well in these pre-amplification days, and his songwriting. He wasn't a Kern or a Gershwin or a Berlin, but he could write the kind of tunes that sold by the hundred thousand on those heavy, brittle 78 rpm records.

He was no sooner signed up as part of the Whiteman Rhythm Boys than he had a new song ready for the outfit; it was called "Mississippi Mud". He couldn't have known that in time it would stand out as the first Bing Crosby tune a generation of fans would remember. Certainly it would be more clearly remembered than "I've Got The Girl" — although it was easier to accept that Bing Crosby had got the girl than to imagine him wallowing in Mississippi Mud. But Bing and the Rhythm Boys sang it on the first disc they recorded away from the Whiteman machine. Although they still retained "Pop's" name, they now had their own independent contract with the prestigious Victor label.

Bing loved the perks and the fame the Paul Whiteman Rhythm Boys brought him. Fourteen million people listened to the *Old Gold Paul Whiteman Hour*, the CBC show sponsored by Old Gold tobacco, which was enough to make him, and the other boys, much sought after by plenty of attractive women about town. The team was earning more than $300 a week each now, a fabulous amount for the late 1920s. This meant that he could wine, dine and bed these fans in a manner to which he was prepared to become fully accustomed. Then afterwards, there was always enough left over for a few bottles of the hard stuff.

The fact that this was in the middle of the Prohibition era does not appear to have made much of an impact, although before long that sort of indifference would land him in serious trouble. There was also plenty of cash for gambling, the Crosby disease.

There is no doubt that Bing was the one who lived it up more than any of his partners. As a result, the other boys frequently found themselves "mugging it up" to hide the fact that Crosby had missed a train or was unable to distinguish between a songsheet and the label of a bottle of Scotch.

Whiteman liked Bing and appreciated his talent and agreed that his three Rhythm Boys had a wonderful rapport with his audiences. They did everything the rest of the band did — performed their own act and sat in with the orchestra to make it look bigger than it actually was. (Bing was given a violin to "play" — one with rubber strings, so that there was no risk he would actually produce a note of any kind.)

But Whiteman knew that he could also be a liability. Pops told him: "Jeez, I've got to do something about you, you're lousing up my band." He also knew that he and the other boys could also be a useful asset. When the Whiteman band played in the Broadway show *Lucky*, the Rhythm Boys were featured along with the others — on stage.

They even recorded "Makin' Whoopee" for Columbia, switching labels at about the same time as Whiteman did. But Pops still wasn't happy with their behaviour. When the orchestra was booked for a tour, the Paul Whiteman Rhythm Boys were not included. Instead, Whiteman sent them out on their own for the show business equivalent of a train ride to Siberia: a 45-week stint touring the country as a vaudeville act.

But was it really that? It has always been popularly assumed that this was some kind of punishment, visited by Whiteman on his recalcitrant young performer. Nevertheless, it does seem unlikely that he would cut off his nose to spite his face. In those days, big outfits like Whiteman's used every available outlet to exploit their talent.

The Rhythm Boys had signed a contract with him and were, therefore, professionally speaking, his property. By all accounts, none of the Rhythm Boys seems to have minded going out on the road in this way. As far as Bing himself was concerned, it was a great opportunity to have a good time, a chance to get into golf in a serious way, more gambling, more drinking, more girls. If

33

sailors had girls in every port, Bing Crosby had them waiting for him in the wings of every vaudeville theatre from New York to Los Angeles.

The girls were always there for him — chorus girls, girls who worked at typewriters and girls who stood behind store counters. Only once did he consider that he had entered into an alliance that was a bit too rich for his blood. She was a socialite-millionairess living in Akron, Ohio, who he thought would expect more than he was prepared to deliver.

In Chicago, he fell in love with a girl called Peggy Bernier, who was starring in *Good News*. The Bad News was that she wasn't interested in him. But before the show's run was finished, she left the cast. Her place was taken by a pretty young actress named Dixie Lee. Bing took little notice of her, this time.

Vaudeville time duly served, the Paul Whiteman Rhythm Boys were back working with their employer and his orchestra — full time. It was in 1929 that the real break came his way. Whiteman was signed by Universal studios to make a movie — to be called *The King Of Jazz*.

CHAPTER
FIVE

The King of Jazz

Whiteman had been calling himself "the King Of Jazz" for years — although what he played was much more a harbinger of swing than pure jazz. It was big-band jazz concerts that had people stamping their feet and dancing in the aisles at the close of the decade they were calling the "Roaring Twenties". Nothing roared more than the kind of music played by the Whiteman band, with its instrumentalists like Bix Beiderbecke and the guitarist Eddie Lang, who would later work with Bing, and whom Crosby called "the greatest one of his craft who ever lived".

More than that, jazz was the word that got the Hollywood juices going. *The Jazz Singer* — also a title that used the word "jazz" rather liberally — had set the country and the film industry aflame and consigned the silent movie to the scrap heap. All the other studios were now themselves wiring for sound — and trying to find ways of outdoing the Warner Brothers in the field they had pioneered.

Both *The Jazz Singer* and Jolson's follow-up movie, *The Singing Fool*, were only partly talking movies. Carl Laemellae, the pint-sized boss of Universal, was determined to go at least three stages better. His studio's new film would be totally all-singing, all-dancing, all-talking and then, what's more, would be made partly in colour — even if the colour he had available to him was a blurring shadow of what the Technicolor process would later produce. It was more a splurge than a splash.

Pops set about selling the movie with all the panache of a fairground barker. It was Universal's idea to bring Old Gold into the promotional stakes. It made a great deal of sense, they reasoned, to cash in on the popularity of the radio show. The fan magazines, newspapers and early newsreels had never been happier than when they saw the Old Gold Paul Whiteman Special leave New York's Grand Central Station for the West Coast.

Every member of the Whiteman ensemble had his own private apartment on the squeaky-clean, highly polished train that had been painted shimmering gold for the journey. When it drew into Los Angeles' Union Station, there were cars waiting for them, provided by a local Ford agent, each bearing the Paul Whiteman logo. If only the time spent on the movie itself equalled the ballyhoo surrounding it.

Months — and thousands of dollars — were spent trying to firm up a script that was constantly being rewritten. Screen and sound tests — a totally novel concept — went on for month after month. So much time was wasted that Bing went round the other Hollywood studios himself, making a series of screen tests on his own. His name and his talent meant studios were prepared to spend about $70,000 giving him the tests, but they never amounted to anything, as far as he was concerned. All that he got were salvos of advice, some suggesting he lose weight and pin back his protruding ears.

Bing consoled himself with an introduction to the Lakeside Country Club next to the Universal lot — not dreaming that one day he would be its champion. He also introduced himself to another local institution — the jail.

He was driving his sponsored Ford along Hollywood Boulevard towards the Roosevelt Hotel — then just about the smartest hostelry serving the movie community — when a car rear-ended him. The girl — there was always a girl — with him was thrown through the windscreen on to the road, from which Bing lifted her, blood-stained and unconscious, and carried her into the hotel foyer.

Surprisingly, the girl wasn't seriously hurt. But Bing's pride — and his civic reputation — was. The police smelt alcohol on his breath, arrested him and locked him up for the night. It was up to Whiteman to provide the bail.

Soon afterwards, the band was sent packing back to New York; Whiteman couldn't wait any longer for filming to begin. They fulfilled a full schedule of gigs until, finally, the word was given. *The King Of Jazz* was ready to go into production.

They came back to Los Angeles, Bing was promptly arrested, appeared in court — and then jailed. The judge saw it as his big opportunity to put the Hollywood hoi polloi in their place. "Haven't you heard of Prohibition?" asked the judge. "No one seems to take much notice of that," Crosby replied. The judge said that he did take notice of it and ordered Bing to be taken to the cells.

Whiteman used all his considerable weight to get his singer released. In the end, a compromise was reached: he could get out during the day to work on the film, but would have to return to the lock-up at night. It was under these restraints that Paul Whiteman's Rhythm Boys performed "A Bench In The Park". But Crosby's jailing meant that the big number for which he had been slated, "Song Of The Dawn", went now to John Bowles.

Bing, however, did get his solo chance. He made his first record on his own, "Just One More Chance". It was a chance worth taking and it became the first Crosby classic. For years the record was hardly ever off the airwaves.

Once Bing was released, the Paul Whiteman Rhythm Boys played in Los Angeles nightclubs after their days at the studios. They were a hit at the Montmartre Café on Hollywood Boulevard. Then, they were booked in at the Cocoanut Grove, the smartest nighterie in the film capital. There, they were an instant sell-out. Bing didn't just sing from the stage, he went out into the audience — in case they couldn't hear him over the concerted din of plates being crashed, cutlery being shuffled and glasses clinked.

At this point, Bing Crosby and the Paul Whiteman Rhythm Boys left the man who had founded their fame. Now they were just the Rhythm Boys. It was also the moment at which Bing met Dixie Lee again.

CHAPTER
SIX

Dixie

It didn't look like a romance made in any kind of heaven. Wilma Winifred Wyatt had the new name of Dixie and was a promising young actress who now had a contract with Fox, the company that had not only grabbed at the opportunities of the "talkie" era, but had gone a stage further than anyone else: their famed Movietone system was the first to put sound on film. Nobody was saying that putting Dixie's voice on to that soundtrack was going to make Fox millions, but she was a pleasant enough singer with a sexy enough voice, who had once understudied the "Love Me Or Leave Me" girl Ruth Etting. The face of the 19-year-old in the background of a movie poster was reckoned to at least help bring in the customers. In *The Fox Movietone Follies of 1929*, she was the perfect advertisement. In the case of the film *The Big Party*, there was evidence that young men came just to see her.

On the other hand, Mr Crosby was widely talked of as a small-time singer who was doing very nicely for himself at the moment, but he did not seem destined for greater things. Sure, he had the girls running after him, but any fly-by-night performer had that. Nobody was going to stay loyal to him. Why should they? There was nothing very special about him. Was there? Dixie was even heard to have called him, with a nice alliteration, a "bumptious baritone".

But there were aphrodisiac qualities in a man who could stand in front of an orchestra with a megaphone in his hand. And there was also his gift of the gab. He didn't just ask for a date. Instead he wondered if they would care to share his perambulations around the neighbourhood, which was simply music to some women's ears.

Bing had been infatuated with Dixie ever since the night of their second introduction at the Cocoanut Grove. The Rhythm Boys were now playing with the famous Gus Arnheim orchestra. Matty Malneck had a table at the Grove, which was made famous by the giant mock coconut palms brought into the club at the Ambassador Hotel (having served their time as props for a Rudolph Valentino film). Malneck had brought a friend there for the evening and the friend brought Dixie. This time she softened.

The romance was soon the talk of the town, particularly among those who had read stories about Dixie and believed her own publicity. Fox were worried. They didn't like the idea of one of their girls of promise being tied down to a nobody. It was an age when studios liked to pair off their stars with other stars. It was good publicity. It was also a question of reputation: if Dixie went steady with a no-good, what did that say about her?

But she became infatuated, too. The only question in her mind was the Crosby lifestyle, a factor that had been giving not a little worry to the old folks in Spokane and was beginning to make both Al Rinker and Harry Berris anxious, too. Bing wasn't exactly a reliable partner. Maybe Dixie could straighten him out. She wasn't sure. This was a man, she said, who spent twice as much as he earned and, where she came from in Tennessee, that was not just imprudent, it was a recipe for disaster.

Bing, though, was willing to be persuaded to change all that — just so long as Dixie changed *her* mind and married him. To everyone's surprise, not least that of Messrs Rinker and Berris, she said yes.

Bing and Dixie were married on 30 September 1930 at the Blessed Sacrament Church on Hollywood Boulevard (one of the more attractive streets in the film capital before it was overtaken by sleaze).

The second surprise for the other two Rhythm Boys was that they weren't invited. A select few had a telephone call that morning to put on their best suits and dresses and hop over to the church. That, though, was in character. The take-it-nice-and-easy singer wasn't going to let a little thing like a wedding make him get serious.

The people at Fox were now even more unhappy. It might well have been an aggrieved publicist who spread the word to the trade press that things were on a disaster course. He persuaded a headline writer to record the fact that an "obscure" young singer was marrying one of their "stars". One report went so far as to head their story: "Well-Known Fox Movie Star Marries Bing Croveny". That was fame — particularly for a man who was listed in the studio casting directors' books under the heading of "comedian".

Friends had also joined the studio in trying to talk her out of the wedding. Bing was to recall: "But she married me, anyhow. One of the things they threw at Dixie was that she'd have to support me for the rest of my life."

It certainly didn't help Bing's relationship with Berris and Rinker, although they stayed loyal — more loyal than Crosby was to them. They happily sat in for him when mysteriously Bing failed to turn up for one of their shows at the Cocoanut Grove. Once, they substituted for him for three days. Bing was ill, they told the Grove owner Abe Frank, and he reluctantly accepted it, although it was hard for him to contain his anger at the kind of unprofessional behaviour he found difficult to tolerate. He must have known that Crosby was either in Mexico gambling, playing golf or on a drinking bender, but he wanted him back.

Bing's marriage had attracted a great deal of publicity, so when he *did* show, you couldn't get a table in the place. And then there was that voice. He might be a fly-by-night five-minute wonder, but those five minutes were becoming exciting. Even though Frank thought Crosby would never get anywhere — nobody thought he was ever going to make it — the customers liked that voice they were hearing for the first time whenever he did one of his solos.

Naturally, the other two didn't like it, but they put up with it — as they knew Dixie would have to do. They felt more sorry for her than they did for themselves. She was the meal ticket and she was the one who would have to constantly bail him out of trouble.

And then it happened. Bing was absent from the

Grove for another three days. Abe Frank heard that he had been throwing the dice in Mexico and decided he had had enough. Actually, it seems that Bing was doing something much more innocent, if equally unprofessional. He was out of town — gone fishing, a marvellous foretaste of his hit of that name with Louis Armstrong. He made money out of that 1951 record but he lost his job through that 1931 excursion.

Not just Bing: the Rhythm Boys were out. What was more, Frank was going to take all the revenge he had at his disposal. As any self-respecting nightclub owner would, he had contacts. Now he called them in. It only took a phone conversation with the American Federation of Musicians to get Bing Crosby effectively blacklisted. No musician would play with him. As for the Rhythm Boys, they were finished. It was all over.

CHAPTER
SEVEN

Back in Business

His career wasn't the only thing that was finished — his marriage was, too. A year later Dixie had enough and filed for divorce. But then two things happened. For reasons no one has yet been able to fully explain, Bing Crosby managed to persuade the musicians' union to allow him to work again. (He was never a union member but by banning others from working with him they had brought his career to a standstill.) There are theories as to how Bing got back in their favour, he either paid a hefty fine to the union or he paid compensation to Abe Frank. A five-figure settlement has been talked of but never proven.

Then he talked Dixie into having him back, too. Dixie took Bing back because she loved him. It was as simple as that. She also knew that, for all his problems, he cared about her. His return to the business was thanks to two men. Everett, his elder brother, who had been selling trucks for a living, was now officially his manager, lending a sober, guiding hand to the Crosby career. But it was a lawyer named Roger Marchetti hovering in the background who, according to some people in the business, was the real Crosby saviour.

There doesn't seem much doubt that Marchetti was the man responsible for a totally unexpected development. Bing Crosby, the man who couldn't get work just a few weeks before, was now starring in a film, which was going on release at just about the time that his status in the industry had so mysteriously been restored.

He had already made a couple of movies since *The King Of Jazz*, for the Pathe organization. One was called *Check And Double Check*, with Amos and Andy. It made little noise. A second film, *Ripstitch The Tailor*, was never released and no copies survive. It might very well have been the end of the Crosby movie career if this new opportunity had not arisen.

It wasn't going to be a product of one of the big companies. Educational Studios, where the movie was shot, couldn't match the products of any of the big moguls and certainly were not competitors of Dixie Lee's bosses, Fox. In fact, the person in charge was probably the least likely to ever want to make a film musical. As for his films being educational — say custard pies and you said Mack Sennett.

But it was a gamble that paid off. Bing sang a new song for the Sennett film, a number that Harry Berris wrote for him called "I Surrender, Dear", which the old Keystone Kops producer thought was so good, it should be the title of the film. *I Surrender, Dear* was just two reels long, but word of the movie spread and before long people all over America were looking for the theatres that featured the short as part of its programme.

Bing's fee for the film? $750. Not much for a film star, even for 1931, but enough for Bing to agree to sign a contract to make five more for Sennett.

There was another development: Bing's record went as close to top of the pops as it was possible to get. So did another featured in the movie, "Out Of Nowhere". The song was written by the man who later became musical director of MGM, Johnny Green. "I couldn't believe what Crosby did for that song," he was to tell me. "Like everyone else, I didn't exactly rate him as a great singer or a great personality. But somehow, there was a style there I hadn't imagined."

And it was that word "style" that began to be identified with the way Bing sang. It didn't sound the same as the way everyone else sang. Not that Bing himself took much credit for it. "It just happened," he told me. "I never thought I had more than a passable voice."

Was that false modesty? No. It was exactly what he thought of his vocal talents. To attempt a new style would have taken hard work and Crosby wasn't convinced he needed to work at anything. It is probable that it was by chance rather than design that his voice delighted so many people.

His two ex-partners were not going to be so lucky. Berris went on writing songs, a lot of them for Bing. Al Rinker became a radio producer and neither of them would ever say a bad word about their fellow Rhythm Boy — at least not for publication.

In November 1931, Bing was starring on his own at New York's Paramount Theatre — the very place from which the Rhythm Boys had been so unceremoniously expelled. This time, there was no suggestion of his being unable to get his voice across to the audience. Indeed, it was made easier for him — by singing from an overhead crane. That came after being wheeled out on to the stage in a flower-decked cart. He not only survived the engagement, he was the biggest sensation the theatre had had for its four daily shows — a record only broken by that young upstart Frank Sinatra ten years later.

One night, the crane broke and Bing was left hanging over the audience — singing to a crowd of drunken sailors who struggled to pull off Bing's shoes and socks while he sang his heart out. It was the first demonstration of Crosby actually working for his applause.

He may have had another incentive to do well. While he was starring at the New York Paramount, Russ Colombo was at its "poor" brother theatre — the Paramount, Brooklyn. No one knows for how long the rivalry between Crosby and Colombo would have gone on. Colombo was very popular, but he didn't have Bing's stage presence, his sense of humour, his personality (even though many people thought their voices were totally interchangeable).

Bing would say charitably that there was room for them both, but that was in retrospect. No one could put their competition to the test of years. At the height of his success, Colombo was at a friend's house, examining his collection of rare Civil War-vintage guns. A gun went off, lodging a lead ball into the singer's left eye. He was dead within an hour.

Rudy Vallee, star of the *Fleishmann Hour*, was now Crosby's only rival, but the films in which Bing had appeared showed that audiences liked him better. Now that he was performing vocal gymnastics with that high baritone of his, the world was his for the taking.

There was a contract for a CBS radio programme, arranged by Everett or Marchetti. But on the night of the first broadcast, there was no Bing and no transmission. Crosby sent word that he had lost his voice. A story was published that he had consulted doctors who recommended surgery but that he had turned it down because they couldn't guarantee that it would leave his voice unchanged. There were nodes on his vocal cords and, they said, they were responsible for what was now being recognized as the distinctive Crosby sound. It would be a story that would last for another half century. Except that there are tales that Bing was actually drinking — so heavily that he was virtually paralytic.

The following week, Bing did make it up to the microphone. He was paid $600 a week for a nightly 15-minute show. The radio series had followed one another, one sponsored by Cremo cigars, then one for the Los Angeles-based Leroy Diamond Company, followed by a stint for Woodbury Soap, the programme that would later be sponsoring a certain Mr Bob Hope.

Before long, he was the star of the *Chesterfield Hour*, too. But the Bing Crosby who was attracting something like 20 million listeners a week to his shows was also now a film star. Either Everett or Marchetti — both would later be given credit for the move — had had a meeting with Adolph Zukor, head of Paramount Pictures. He was making a new film, 1932's *The Big Broadcast*. He wanted Crosby for one of the big parts.

The picture had started off by being called *Wild Waves* and for a brief time was going to be *The Crooner* — the job description being handed now to all the young men who sang in what was the Crosby style.

There was still competition for the title role as well as of the status of being The Crooner. Rudy Vallee was said to have been in line for the *Big Broadcast* role, as he was for Bing's position in the pop world. The papers dubbed their rivalry the "Battle of the Baritones", although the singers claimed there was no feud — indeed Vallee later went on record to say that Bing was the best of them all.

Certainly, Crosby was very much the man of his times. His recording of the Depression anthem, "Brother Can You Spare A Dime?", became not only a Crosby standard, but also a perfect commentary on the age when formerly successful businessmen were lining up at street soup kitchens for food.

In reality, Crosby was just one of a roster of players in *The Big Broadcast*, along with George Burns and Gracie Allen, the Mills Brothers, the Boswell Sisters and Arthur Tracy, "the Street Singer". But Bing was the one who counted. Reviewers described his performance in the film as though recording the arrival of a complete unknown.

But neither film nor the radio shows constituted a real sea-change in Bing's career. They didn't set him apart from all the other people who made movies or sang on the radio. It was the big heavy black platters that went round at 78 rpm which were causing a revolution in home entertainment. "Where The Blue Of The Night Meets The Gold Of The Day" was now his theme song, much to the displeasure of Harry Berris, who said Bing had promised he would use "I Surrender, Dear". When it was committed to 78 it became an instant big seller, on the back of both the radio publicity and the movie's success.

Bing Crosby, with his now-habitual apparent lack of effort, and with the help of a character waiting in the wings, was on his way to becoming one of the most important artists in recording history.

CHAPTER
EIGHT

Ski Slopes And Corsets

Jack Kapp was a record mogul, although the phrase was not used at the time any more then "standards" or "flipsides". His big move was to go into business with the English Sir Edward Lewis and set up a new American company in association with his British Decca label. Kapp knew Bing and his drawing power as a recording artist. Crosby was at the time making his discs on the Brunswick label, where Kapp was director of recording. When Kapp left Brunswick to start Decca, he took Bing with him. The very first issue on the new blue label was Bing Crosby singing "Just A-Wearyin' For You" and "I Love You Truly".

"Just A-Wearyin'" was to become a Crosby classic, a future standard. That was the kind of business Decca and Crosby would be in. Bing was going to make the label the launch pad for a whole swathe of songs that would for ever after be identified with him — songs that would be remembered long after most people could recall where and when they had first heard them.

But that wasn't all there was to that relationship between singer and label. Kapp realized that people were buying Bing's records more for his voice than for many of the songs he sang. He got Bing started on a career of recording anything that took his fancy — Kapp's fancy, that is.

Yes, there would be the tunes both men hoped would become classics. But there would be semi-folksongs, too — like "Just A-Wearyin'" — religious tunes, Irish tunes, spirituals, comedy songs. "Kapp had the ideas and I figured he knew his business — so I recorded what he told me to," Bing told me shortly before his death.

It was a good arrangement; one that would sell those 400 million discs of 4,000 different recordings. At one time there would be at least two sides of Crosby songs issued every week; sometimes a great many more. He was as popular in Britain as he was in America. There, the records were sold under the Brunswick label which Kapp had left behind in New York. (British Decca marketed local artists.)

Decca was scooping up a whole swathe of other top entertainers like Al Jolson and Guy Lombardo, but Bing Crosby was now their Big Star. Other artists had done well out of records; Crosby was the first musician to be primarily a recording artist and the first to make the business of selling them into an art form.

Decca appreciated his value from the word go. But they worried about getting their man's full attention. After all, he was a star of films and radio programmes as well as a disc maker. Kapp had the answer to that, too. He built a recording studio specially for Bing's use, just outside the Paramount lot.

Zukor had been delighted with *The Big Broadcast*, which spawned a series of movies bearing that title — a year would be added to new *Big Broadcast* movies until the genre had gone its full stretch in 1938 with the first major film starring Bob Hope.

Crosby was under contract to Paramount, for whom he would make more than fifty movies; quite an achievement considering he wasn't principally a film actor. But he was not beyond giving the studio its share of Crosby-style problems, which didn't surprise anyone who knew the way Bing had formerly led his life. He did try to behave himself while making his second Paramount film, *College Humor* ("A light frothy musical that doesn't give customers much of a mental workout," said *Variety*), but there was still trouble.

The film co-starred Mary Carlisle, Jack Oakie, George Burns and Gracie Allen. Burns told me: "Bing was a strange fellow. Very cold. He didn't want to socialize. He might have had a girl because he always wanted to get away. But I don't think he did. I don't think he wanted to get back to Dixie, either. I think he just liked being alone — and drinking." It was a revealing observation.

As long as Crosby turned up on the set when required, Zukor and the other bosses at Paramount didn't seem to worry too much. They ignored his other peccadilloes. The trouble came when, in the middle of filming *College Humor*, Bing said he had had enough of having to stick his protruding ears back with tape and gave it up as a bad job. Observant viewers, therefore, were able to see Bing with big ears in one scene and hardly visible ones in the next; only for it to be back to old big ears again. No one at the studio seemed to bother. They certainly didn't try to do it again.

Playing golf was to be more of a problem. Bing was plainly happier at Lakeside than he was on the Paramount lot. He escaped one day to take part in the 1932 US Open Golf championship — under an assumed name; when his true identity was discovered he was instantly disqualified.

Bing had no desire to change his name as far as his ever-burgeoning professional career was concerned. Later in 1932, it was emblazoned on the marquee over the Capitol Theatre in New York. He was in vaudeville again, making an indecent amount of money and showing off to a brash young performer who was on the bill, too. His name was Bob Hope.

They took note of each other, saw that critics took note, too, and started talking about each other in public, gradually at first, but before long none of their radio shows were without mention of the other man. Bing made outrageous comments about Bob's nose — the "ski slope", as it came to be called — and Hope referred to the Crosby ears and girth. He may or may not have known that Bing was now having to wear a corset under his suits.

By most accounts, the Crosby home at this time resembled scenes from *Who's Afraid Of Virginia Woolf?*, with charge and counter charge resounding from room to room in the Hollywood house. Bing, in a perfect demonstration of a pot calling a kettle black, hated the fact that Dixie drank. He forgot that there had to be a reason for her behaviour. His actress wife was actually pitifully shy, and Bing's refusal to appreciate this was an ongoing source of hurt for her.

The marriage would have ended by now, in true Hollywood style, had Dixie not announced that she was pregnant. In 1933, she gave birth to their first son, Gary, whom they named after Bing's friend Gary Cooper. A year later, Philip and Dennis, the Crosby twins were born.

CHAPTER
NINE

The Terpsichorean Trail

On the surface, everything was looking perfect in the Bing-Dixie household. Fan magazines showed the baby Crosbys and their parents looking radiantly happy. Bing with a hat covering his baldness, a pipe in his mouth, every bit the character he was already making famous in his films. If, in *College Humor*, he looked a bit pudgy and mature for a university story, no one said so. No director had yet thought it necessary to give him a story in one of his movies; at that stage in his career, no one thought he could do more than warble a few of his songs and play himself. But those fan magazines really did love him.

However, they kept quiet about what everyone in the film business knew: Bing was in the midst of a steamy affair with a dancer. Furthermore, what very few people knew — and what it took his sons at least two generations to reveal — was that the new father would turn into a martinet. He punished the little children severely when they were naughty. As they grew older, the beatings got harder. Dixie was frequently distraught but there was nothing she could do. Bing was away more and more, making promotional tours for all those movies in which he showed what a good guy he always was.

Psychiatrists have pondered for more than a century about people like Bing. "Ah," you can hear them thinking, "he must have had a very painful childhood, beaten by his own father, taking out all those old pains and frustrations on a father substitute, a close male relative, any one of his sons." Sorry to disappoint those gentlemen as they sit by their couches. There is no evidence whatsoever to back up that theory. By all accounts, the Crosbys of Spokane were a happy, devoted family. The one incontrovertible fact is that Bing had a cruel streak in him. Too many people point to that to leave the matter in doubt. Was he unhappy about his marriage? Very likely. Did he resent the fact that the boys were growing up in their mother's image? Probably. It also seems probable that the younger Crosbys were convenient dogs to kick when things were going wrong. The lungs that produced the magic voice were the engine for his lost temper.

Yet there was another side to the story. Bing could be nice to people. He was generous to his children when he was in the mood and could often follow a severe beating with an ice cream. His attitude to his manager seemed similar. Now established as a big star on his own, he saw no need to have an organizer for his career, other than Everett, whom he could easily manipulate. He fired Roger Marchetti, the man who had given him most of his big breaks, because, he said, he was tired of paying him 20 per cent commission on all that he earned.

After all, the only problems he now faced were knowing what offers he had to turn down. There was so much work flooding his way, so many young songwriters like Johnny Mercer and Hoagy Carmichael wanting to write for him. There were always groups like the Mills Brothers who wanted to "adopt" him for their new records. And there were up and coming combinations who wanted him, too. He knew that the fresh, young voices of the Andrews Sisters and the Boswell Sisters made him sound as good as he made them seem.

Films were becoming more and more important and as the polls in the fan magazines indicated, he was becoming more and more popular, too. He was still playing himself, wearing a white-topped cap and puffing his pipe in between singing whatever was likely to sell most records in the months that followed the opening. *College Humor* was followed by *Too Much Harmony*, something that could never be said either of Bing's singing or his private life.

Then came *Going Hollywood*, which Bing had already done, of course. But he hadn't done it like that before. He was now working for MGM, "loaned" to the studio by Paramount for more money than he himself was going to earn. This was more the inspiration of the newspaper magnate William Randolph Hearst than Louis B. Mayer.

It was also spending the publisher's money. Hearst wanted his paramour Marion Davies to make a movie and had read in his papers that Crosby was about the biggest name around. He wanted Bing to star opposite his girlfriend and make her look good. Mayer agreed and the film was made — a not very good film, it has to be said.

The studio found a titillating subject: a crooner chased by a girl who likes to pretend she is a French maid. It sounded like a farce, but turned out to be farcical — both in the making and in the end product. That the respected director Raoul Walsh got involved is even more surprising than that Bing took the easy option and said yes. *Variety* said of it: "Lavishly produced musical with everything but a story."

We're Not Dressing, which included Bing's big hit "Love Thy Neighbour", was more successful and made him happier. He was back at Paramount, where he was now regarded as king of the lot. The movie co-starred the delectable Carole Lombard. Burns and Allen and Ethel Merman were in it, too. The story, based on J. M. Barrie's *The Admirable Crichton*, was one of the best things he did in those inter-war days.

Anyone involved in the film's making would have witnessed one of the high points of their entire professional careers: Bing getting into a physical fight with his co-star. A scene called for Bing to slap Carol's face. She hated the idea and spent days worrying about it, doing her best to get the scene changed, to no avail. She showed up for filming, and as the moment approached prepared herself for the slap.

But nobody was prepared for her reaction. As though she had just been struck in a real lovers' tiff, she hit back — so viciously that she had to be pulled off by studio guards. She kicked Bing in the stomach, tore at his clothes and was so heavy-handed his toupee fell off. Screaming hysterically, she was dragged off.

That moment, trimmed for the public, would have been the most notable thing about an inconsequential film. It was followed by a couple of even more indifferent offerings, *She Loves Me Not* and *Here Is My Heart*, and then by Bing's first foray into costume drama, *Mississippi*. Surprise, surprise, he played a riverboat singer. *Two For Tonight* and *The Big Broadcast Of 1936* followed (he couldn't resist the chance to revisit his big break movie).

Then there was *Anything Goes*, with Ethel Merman and Charlie Ruggles. It was the best musical of the period. It couldn't help being that with the Cole Porter score that included the title song as well as "You're The Top" and "I Get A Kick Out Of You". *Rhythm On The Range* and *Pennies From Heaven* (in which Bing sang, guess what . . .) came next and deserve to be forgotten just as *Anything Goes* ought to be remembered. But most of these movies were merely vehicles for the stars and their songs.

By this time, he had added horse racing to his leisurely obsessions. It was another activity to take him away from his wife (now a full time housewife after her last film *Love In Bloom*) and children. In 1935, having already indulged this passion by buying "Zombie", his first ever racehorse, he went a stage further: he bought a racetrack.

Del Mar, on the Californian coast between San Diego and Santa Monica, was to become the track of the stars — as much because he owned it with his partner Pat

O'Brien as for the course and adjoining clubhouse. Both places exercised an almost religious pull on the two actors who might have regarded the sentiment as sacrilege — since they both enjoyed playing priests.

They had to sell stock in the track before the project could be realized but the Crosby-O'Brien connection brought in the punters. Bing stamped his own personality on the place from the word go by recording a song dedicated to the establishment. For more than ten years, Bing's musical version of the track's motto "Where The Turf Meets The Surf" was played over the loudspeakers at the beginning of every race meeting. People queuing up to place a bet said it helped relieve the tension of waiting for the subsequent broadcasts over those loudspeakers — the race commentary which told them they had lost their stake.

Bing's interest in the First National Bank Of Hollywood was seen by some as a safer investment. But there were other gambles in Bing's life, like continuing his marriage to Dixie Lee. She was, they said, more under the influence of alcohol than she was of her husband, but nevertheless she gave him their fourth son, Lindsay, in January 1938. Another gamble was knowing how to control his career when it hit the odd stumbling block.

He had gone on to star in what was regarded as the top variety show on American radio, the *Kraft Music Hall*, selling cheese between songs (or at least the announcer would do the selling; Bing tried his best to steer away from the commercials). His band-leader was Jimmy Dorsey, as big as it was possible to get at the end of the

1930s (along with Tommy Dorsey, who was struggling with young Mr Sinatra). But there was a clash of artistic temperament, which is never surprising when two men think they are both the stars of the operation.

Bing's solution was to get rid of Dorsey and hire a man who was more a musician than a star and who would never constitute a threat to his own billing. It was a wise move. The man he chose was John Scott Trotter, whose name would come second on Bing Crosby records for the next 20 years and who was virtually never absent from a Crosby broadcast.

He was a large, quiet man who never said anything more threatening than a stern "Gentlemen!" Bing said he was the greatest gourmet he ever knew. But there was more to Scott Trotter than that. He was a huge musical influence on Bing; one who had a similar sort of effect on the way Crosby sang as Nelson Riddle was to have on the Sinatra performing style 16 years later. Like Riddle with Sinatra, Trotter didn't change the Crosby voice, but rather the way he used it, his style. The orchestrations sounded different, with emphasis placed on harmonies instead of melody, and so Bing himself sounded different. He was no longer blown over by trumpets and trombones. Now, more than before, Bing was able to experiment with the songs he sang. He enjoyed his "boo-boo-be-boos" in between phrases, which allowed him to drop a register or two when he thought the occasion demanded. It would be a style that would stay with him for ever after.

There were guests on the radio programmes, and always Bing introduced them by giving full rein to his vocabulary and the tricks he played with it. A visit to the *Kraft Music Hall* by Fred Astaire would be greeted by Bing saying to his orchestra leader: "Now, John Scott [it was always "John Scott" to him] let's take a trip down the terpsichorean trail."

So, he brought this style to bear across his performances. With Bing in charge of the *Hall*, it became more important than ever and Bing Crosby could do what he wanted with it. When, in 1938, Bing was offered an honorary doctorate by his alma mater, Gonzaga University in Spokane, he had the answer to double-booking with which nobody could argue — least of all Kraft, who would benefit from the publicity. He took the show to Spokane and made the programme from there, which was very unusual indeed at the time.

Every week, there were new songs, which helped Crosby's reputation for being able to sing anything, and usually did.

And on the movie screen, fans — mostly women — waited to hear what the new hit would be, knowing full well that they would be hearing it more than once on his radio programmes or those of other stars, on which he was always a welcome guest. Once the songs had been heard on the radio, and after a highly productive airing on the screen, there was a guarantee that Decca would be pulling out all the stops to sell them on record.

A man like Bing Crosby, who still didn't like working hard, had it all made. There seemed no reason to change his highly successful lifestyle, either professionally or on the golf course or at the racetrack.

Then in 1939 came an offer that would add a totally new dimension to his career. He was invited to join up with the young comedian with whom he had jousted a few years before. He and Bob Hope were going to make a film. It was originally going to be called *Road To Mandalay*. But by the time they arrived on the Paramount lot, the title had been changed.

CHAPTER
TEN

On The Road

No one now doubted that Bing Crosby was America's number one popular vocalist. The fact that in an unguarded moment Bob Hope had described him as the greatest singer in the world didn't do any harm either. But, to date, none of his movies had been so memorable that his name would appear in any reputable history of Hollywood. Thanks to this one film all that was going to change. And how.

He had made movies all through the 1930s. There was one, the 1937 *Waikiki Wedding*, in which Bing's song "Sweet Leilani" won an Oscar (a constantly disputed Academy Award, considering that it beat "They Can't Take That Away From Me" to the honours list).

Except for *Waikiki Wedding* and, perhaps, the 1938 *Sing You Sinners*, a story about a racehorse that featured a junior Donald O'Connor, his movies were forgotten as soon as the audiences had bought the records and played them for the first time. That was the thing with Crosby pictures, the songs frequently lived on, the films never did. *Paris Honeymoon*, *East Side Of Heaven* and *The Star Maker* were perfect examples.

And then came that movie which was not going to be called *Road To Mandalay*. To keep that name would, Paramount decided, create unhelpful associations with Rudyard Kipling — which not only wouldn't exactly bring in the crowds, it could have brought in the family lawyers (who, famously, 15 years later, would make plenty of trouble for Frank Sinatra when he adapted the Kipling verses in his own version of the song).

Paramount had had the project on its stocks for a couple of years. Jack Oakie and Fred MacMurray came to mind at first — and departed swiftly. Then Paramount thought it would be a good vehicle for Burns and Allen, but they had had enough of making inconsequential movies. Who else did Paramount have? Bing might benefit from a change of pace, they thought. He hadn't done much in the way of comedy. Bob Hope was around on the contract list, too — and he was not only good for funny situations, he actually did a little singing.

The notion of combining Hope and Crosby as a movie double-act would prove to be one of the most canny castings in Hollywood history.

Finally making it was the result of a rollercoaster series of decisions. The casting was just one of them. Even changing the title had not been as simple as one would have thought. One bright spark in the Paramount chain of command came up with *Beach Of Dreams*. But fortunately for Hope and Crosby, to say nothing of posterity, those dreams were beached.

No one then could have anticipated that *Road To Singapore* would become more than just a single film. No one was rash enough to predict a sequel, let alone a series — certainly not that it would be the first in the most successful clutch of movies for a generation.

The writers Don Hartman and Frank Butler created an institution. As far as Crosby and Hope were concerned, that institution was called a bank. It was also the first in a collection of comedy movies which converted Bing from being "no more" than a singer into a comedy actor of immense stature.

It wasn't a sure bet for the producers. At best Bing could have been just the crooner in the movie, at worst Hope's sidekick. As it turned out, he was much bigger than either of those things. He ad-libbed as much as did Hope. In fact, he did it so well, he could have been a member of Bob's celebrated joke factory.

There was, of course, a third member of the team who became — or so it seemed, until the very last picture of the series — as indispensable as the pat-a-cake routine (the old nursery game that preceded the villain of the piece being dispatched to some other meaningless role in another Paramount movie). This was, of course, Dorothy Lamour, former Miss New Orleans and occasional cabaret singer (spotted in that role by Bob Hope, with whom she later worked in the *Big Broadcast Of 1938*), who after *Singapore* was hopeful of becoming as popular as her two male sparring partners.

She didn't, it has to be said, like the ad libs. That was a department in which she plainly could not compete and would have complained had she not been aware of her comparative lack of clout. The ad libs would not be her only cause for displeasure.

When the *Road* films were in production, she was as famous as the other two, but made little impact in her subsequent movies. Unlike Bing and Bob, she had no record career to speak of and her only radio performances were limited to guest spots on their shows — which, of course, served to publicize the movies when they were released.

She resented the fact that her own view of herself as an equal partner was never shared by either Hope or Crosby, who seem to have sewn up the whole operation between themselves, while Paramount, who paid their salaries and their bonuses, smiled benignly.

There is certain evidence that Hope was kinder to Dorothy than was Crosby. He was always a sucker for a pretty face and Ms Lamour's face could be as alluring as her bust and hips. Had she agreed to play ball and allow Hope into her bed, it is possible her status might have improved. But she didn't and in any case, Bing, whose womanizing had abated, at least a little, wouldn't have allowed it.

She was excluded from every discussion between the two men, who gave an outward impression that they had been buddies from the cradle, and that nothing could tear them apart. That was never true. Bob was in public more generous about Bing than Crosby ever was about him. They continued to josh with and about each other on their radio shows and did what had to be done for publicity purposes — Bing with reluctance; he said he was in show business to sing, not talk. But at the end of each day they went their separate ways.

Mostly it seems to have had a lot to do with Bing's determination to be a loner. That was a legacy of his Spokane background, where strangers were people to suspect, never to be invited into the bosom of the family. It also grew from a fear that people wanted him for what he was, not who he was — and for his money, which by now was reaching epic proportions. He was almost certainly earning a million dollars a year — a fee he could have achieved by never leaving the recording studio. At the time of the second *Road* film, *Road To Zanzibar*, he was making an average of two sides a week.

There was no suggestion that he would lay down his life for Bob, or for anyone else for that matter. Yet that voice of his was becoming magnetic. It was sounding more mature now, just deep enough to handle the ballads of the day, but without too much bass. The old high tones had vanished.

It was the beginning of Crosby's undisputed reign. He benefited from the fact that his partnership with Bob wasn't permanent. This was not always the case. Usually, a successful combination meant a virtual marriage. Once a couple had become a team, Hollywood liked to keep them that way. Fred Astaire and Ginger Rogers and William Powell and Myrna Loy, in the *Thin Man* series, managed to survive separation but they were the exception. Laurel and Hardy had to be together. Abbott couldn't walk without Costello and, at the end of that decade, it seemed that Martin and Lewis were tied to each other by some kind of umbilical cord (and when they weren't, the results were for a long time disastrous).

It is true that Crosby and Hope were better than both Abbott and Costello and Martin and Lewis. And a greater draw. But they maintained their solo careers for most of the time.

Immediately after *Road To Singapore*, Bing appeared solo in *If I Had My Way*. It was a great cue for a song, if not for a tired story of a vaudevillian. That was followed with *Rhythm On The River*. In this he played a songwriter, who used "ghosts" to write his material. Always a risky subject for a man like him, who supplied a constant supply of signed newspaper articles at this time, pieces that he probably never even saw.

But when *Road To Zanzibar* was finally in the can, Paramount were certain they had on their books a very valuable commodity. Argue with Crosby and there would be trouble. If he wanted to make other pictures, they had to let him get on with it. After *Zanzibar*, he was on distinctly American soil with one of his favourite movies, *Birth Of The Blues*. His co-star in this story of a jazz band in New Orleans was Mary Martin. It was a good combination, especially when the two were joined by Jack Teagarden for "The Waiter, The Porter And The Upstairs Maid" (another classic and another huge hit on record).

The picture did well, but what the crowds really loved was the banter and the ad libs of the *Road* films. (Hope once joked to writer Don Hartman: "If you hear any of your own lines, shout 'Bingo'." The writer was not amused).

In the films, Bing always got the girl. Which, bearing in mind Bing's current determination to behave himself, shows just how unreal the films were. Bing was the brave, adventurous one, Bob the coward. These were conventions designed for films which provided relief from the tensions of those early war years. In fact, Hope had already gone under fire with his shows for the troops but Bing was only just realising he would have to force himself to entertain the forces.

But what was Bing's appeal for the girls in the audience? He may not have put it into practice much — that, too, would have been anathema to the man who didn't want outsiders in his life — but there were stories of women soldiers putting Bing's photographs on the inside of their lockers. They liked him because they dreamed of being serenaded by him. The idea of lying in his arms while he sang "Moonlight Becomes You" drove some of them into swoons. Yet he was the one who, on screen, made love with his hat on (in more than one *Road* film, he wore the famous headgear in bed).

Dixie would have been satisfied with that — except that he was never at home. Merle Oberon would tell the story of the time that Dixie, beautifully dressed and made up, her diamonds glinting, sat in tears at a party. Bing, who was supposed to join her for the event, had just decided not to turn up.

The *Road* films were, as far as she could see, Trips To Escapism. But Bing let no one know that he or his wife had problems. The publicity machine only told the funny stories about the Crosby family. Like the humorous side of the affliction which kept him out of the Army. He was colour blind. Had the early journeys, those to Morocco, Utopia and Rio, which followed the excursions to Singapore and Zanzibar been in colour, audiences might well have spotted a Bing Crosby wearing socks or shoes that didn't exactly match.

There is nothing on record to show that he tried to break the medical barrier and get into the service. But he did say that he thought he could be useful to the Air Force. People with colour blindness could see through the camouflage, he said — a military secret that didn't seem to interest the defence department all that much at the time.

He wasn't blind to the situations in the *Road* films, however — like the time in *Road To Utopia* when he and Bob found themselves tussling with a real bear (which, the following day, bit an arm off its keeper). The two were hiding under a rug. When they poked their heads out, the very real bear greeted them with a very real growl. "We both then had a laundry problem," said Hope afterwards, and no one could be sure if he was joking.

Bing may have had a number of comic lines (usually written in advance, but not always) but he was supposed to be the sensible, sober one. It was left to Bob, standing in a bar in the Yukon while everyone else was partaking of the local gut-rot, to order a glass of lemonade — "in a dirty glass".

In *Road To Morocco*, Bob and Bing were seen in bed having the same dream. They moved from one overhead bubble to the other but even in that it was Hope who was the schlemiel.

Neither of them played the fool in reality, however. There was a sense of rivalry between them the like of which had never been seen even in the cut-throat world of Hollywood. Both decided they wanted an Oscar. Bing set out to get his and, as we shall see, succeeded. Bob never made it. "Academy Award nights are called Passover in my house," he only partly joked.

That was why, in every other field, they competed with each other as if they were a pair of racehorses. Hope, it is true, was never particularly interested in the track. But golf? On the greens, they played against each other as though it were a matter of life or death — no, it was much more important than that.

Bing would before long have his own tournament. Hope followed with one of his own. They both went into real estate — with Bob buying more of the San Fernando Valley than was actually owned by the United States government. Bing did it, too, but he diversified his business interests to include a music publishing outlet and even an electronics company — one which would prove very profitable indeed.

Always, there was the sense that they were looking over their shoulders at each other. Had Irving Berlin yet written his song "Anything You Can Do, I Can Do Better" people might have been forgiven for thinking it had been dedicated to Hope and Crosby. Sometimes, they realized they couldn't do better than go into partnership with each other.

Like many of the things they did, the most successful of their ventures was born on the golf course. They played with a businessman who they didn't know very well, but to whom, in a moment of charity, they decided to give a game.

"This was an old man," Mel Shavelson — Bob's top writer who supplied dozens of routines for the *Road* films — told me. After the game, he remembered, the man said to the pair: "Bob and Bing, you've been very nice to me, but how much do you fellers get for a movie — and how much do you give the government? You're crazy working for Uncle Sam and not keeping anything for yourselves."

As Shavelson remembers: "They got a little suspicious when he asked them to put two thousand dollars in one of his oil wells. Somehow, they agreed to do so. A few months later, Bob called me into his office and showed me the cheque they had received for their share of the man's oil field. A cheque for six million dollars." That was what came from choosing their partners correctly. The man they felt sorry for was the head of the Gilmore Petroleum Company.

It was Bing who came to Bob with another business tip. He had heard that a small firm had found a way of freezing orange juice and then concentrating it ready for packaging on an assembly line. It's common practice these days. The cartons are on the shelf of every supermarket. But when they agreed to almost totally finance Minute Maid, it was a novelty. They put their money where their ambitions were — and orange juice flowed for them like the oil in Mr Gilmore's field and was to be almost as valuable to them as the black stuff was.

As Hope said: "We meshed and we made a nice dollar together." Bing played the innocent. "There are some of my interests that I don't even know I'm interested in." But that was probably not true. He and Bob both had acute commercial antennae.

Those business deals were the usual topics for discussion at the Paramount commissary — probably one of the reasons that Dorothy Lamour was excluded from their table. She was also excluded from their golf.

"Bing was always a better golfer than I," Bob would say. "He came into the studio with his laces untied — because he'd been on the practising tee at Lakeside. He won the championship at our club several times." Ms Lamour couldn't compete with that.

A Paramount contract player, lower down in the pecking order than any of the three stars, told me he felt sorry for her. "She so much wanted to be part of their team," said Anthony Quinn, "that she resented how much she was left out of things."

She was never consulted about the plot or the clothes she had to wear. But there is some evidence to show that Bing was more upset about his wardrobe than she was about hers. He would have been happy to move from scene to scene in an old sports jacket and a pair of threadbare pants. In *Road To Zanzibar* he had to wear silk pantaloons. He was not a happy man.

Dorothy continued to give the impression of being pretty unhappy too (although not about Bob Hope's advances; after she told him she was not interested, he left her alone and sought out less important contract players). But there was nothing she could do about it.

In 1947, Hope and Crosby became full partners with their studio in the latest travel escapade, a then totally revolutionary concept. They each invested a third of the cost of making *Road To Rio* and scooped up the prodigious profits that tumbled in as a result. Dorothy

75

wanted a slice of the action, too — an appeal that caused as big a laugh on the set as any of Bob's gags. The idea of her being an equal was laughable. She was pretty, sexy and a fair actress who had built up a following, but there could have been *Road* films without her. If either Bing or Bob had bowed out, the series would have died.

Bing and his partner were like rockets that went on and on. The *Road* movies provided the fuel.

CHAPTER
ELEVEN

Holiday Inn

If there hadn't been the excitement of the partnership with Hope, the studios might have considered trying to persuade Bing to make a permanent teaming with another huge star — except that Fred Astaire would never have agreed. "I hate that word, 'team'," Astaire once told me. "It always sounds like a pack of horses." He was then referring to Ginger Rogers, but it applied in equal measure to Bing Crosby. However, watching them together in the 1942 film *Holiday Inn* was another of those magical experiences. The songs Bing had to sing — and one song in particular — saw to that. In a way, it was the story of the *Road* films all over again. The day that Crosby agreed to make this movie, he could have had no idea just how vital it would prove to be for his career.

Ostensibly, it was a chance to merge three great talents in a whole swathe of old Irving Berlin tunes. He was America's favourite songwriter, Fred was everyone's favourite dancer and Bing was the country's favourite singer — one who had already recorded most of the Berlin standards like "Always" and "Easter Parade".

Bing played an innkeeper who only opened for the holidays, a perfect platform for all those tunes that Berlin had already produced, like "Easter Parade" and "God Bless America" which was played every year on the Fourth of July as well as on State occasions. For the movie, he wrote "Say It With Firecrackers" for the country's most patriotic festival. Then there was "Let's Start The New Year Right". "Abraham", sung by Bing with a black choir, was there to illustrate Lincoln's birthday. There was also "Happy Holiday", which was a good stand-in for any festival you could choose to mention. The one holiday that had always given Berlin the most trouble was Christmas. There were too many Christmas songs. What else could be said — or sung?

He found the solution in a tune which would begin with Crosby bemoaning the fact that he was spending the holiday in the sunshine of Beverly Hills, instead of at home in the snow-covered north. Bing wasn't sure that he wanted to sing it. Christmas had always been a very important, very religious event in his family's lifestyle and he was reluctant to "commercialize" it. He had said the same thing about "Silent Night" but his own version of the sacred song, very different from almost every other recording of the carol, had sold a million. (Yet he had taken not a cent from it. All the money went to charity because making money from religion was against his principles.)

"White Christmas" did not have the same connotations. It was also to do considerably better.

Bing himself told me that when the first manuscript of the song was shown to him, he had told its writer: "I don't think you need worry about this one, Irving."

Actually, it was a toss up as to who was the more worried, Bing or Berlin, who was known in the business as a walking-talking nervous wreck whenever he had a musical to produce. He was the only composer who threatened to take action should any of his "tunes", as he always called the songs he produced, be parodied. He even had a notice prohibiting parodying printed on all his sheet music. There are stories that Berlin had written the song some years before, but Crosby and others who worked on the film were adamant when I spoke to them that it was brand new.

"I think if he had heard a comedy parody of 'White Christmas' about that time, he'd have gone up the wall," Bing was to tell me. "He'd be in a snit. He just laid down the law. But he was very enthusiastic — and somehow that enthusiasm would be transferred to everyone else. He'd make you share it."

Berlin's enthusiasm certainly didn't come the day he played it over for the first time to the musical director Walter Scharf. "It was as if he were going to have a baby when he was working on that song," Scharf told me. "There he was playing the piano with boxing gloves on. I never saw a man so wrapped up in himself. It was all tremendously traumatic experience for him."

For Bing, nothing was a traumatic experience. He rehearsed and recorded the song in just 18 minutes. He slobbed around the studio in his oldest ill-matching clothes and just waited for it to happen. Of course, he had all those other numbers to sing in the film. "We thought 'Be Careful, It's My Heart' was going to be the big number in this picture," said Scharf.

And then there were the routines he performed with Fred Astaire. "I'll Capture Your Heart" was the perfect example of Berlin's ability to produce a song for particular artists like a tailor making a bespoke suit. "I'll capture your heart, singing," warbled Crosby. "I'll capture your heart dancing," came back Astaire.

Bing even did a dance routine or two. It was hard work, very hard for Bing. "I'll Capture Your Heart" took 36 takes. That was revolutionary for him, the star known as "One-take Crosby". He never saw any reason to do more. Unlike Sinatra, the man they called "One-take Charlie", he didn't make any pretence about losing the inspiration he felt for a scene once the freshness was gone. He just didn't want to do it more than once. His directors knew that, which was why they never argued. He didn't argue either — and that was the trouble. He only had to be slightly unhappy and he'd just put down his props and walk out. If it had been agreed that filming would stop for lunch (or, in his case, for the day) at, say 1.30, then at 1.30, he put on his hat and walked.

Astaire wouldn't stand for that. Everyone I have spoken to over the years about "Twinkletoes" has used the same word about him — including Bing. "He's a perfectionist," Crosby told me.

But the perfectionist didn't expect Bing to dance as well as he did — as if he could. He would have been very upset had he done so. "He dances like I sing," Astaire told me. Which was being unkind — to himself. Berlin said he would rather have Fred sing one of his songs than anyone else. The intonation and phrasing was always so perfect. But he liked Bing, too. He wouldn't have so willingly given him "White Christmas" had he not — although, as Walter Scharf says, "No one thought it was more than a nice enough song, not much else."

That "nice enough song" would turn out to be the best-selling popular song of all time. Some 350 million copies of the tune have been sold, nearly 40 million of them the records that Bing subsequently made. Despite the huge sales of Sir Elton John's tribute to Princess Diana, "Candle In The Wind", Crosby's "White Christmas" remains supreme 56 years later. It was estimated in the 1980s that its sales had finally beaten the number sold over the years — including Bing's own version — of "Silent Night" itself.

Fred Astaire wasn't surprised that "White Christmas" did well. "Bing was just the right person to sing it. Strangely for a song with that theme, it had to be performed reflectively, but without too much emotion. It wouldn't have worked with a great deal of sentiment — and, as we all had learned by then, Bing wasn't the most emotional of people. In fact, a great many of us thought he was pretty cold."

But, as Astaire said, that was precisely what was needed for a song that yearned for the cold. It had a great deal going for it. The Second World War, as far as America was concerned, was now a year old and the idea of dreaming of a white Christmas struck a chord with the American servicemen battling with the intolerable heat of the South Pacific jungles. "I didn't plan that," said Berlin. "It just shows you that inspiration can be anything."

I once asked Berlin if he thought anyone but Crosby could have sung that song with the same sort of impact. "Yes," he said. "I think Fred could have done it just as well. But I'll tell you this, the boys related to Bing. I think they always felt he was part of their own family."

That indeed was it. As for Berlin, competitors noted wryly that he had managed to corner the holiday market for all time. They didn't yet know that the film's title would before long be adopted by a leading hotel chain, but they did see the impact it was having on contemporary audiences.

"I think this song has the chance of being the 'Tipperary' of the Second World War," Bing said when it was aired on the Hit Parade programme for the first time — the first indication that it was going to be special. That was one of the frustrations of the music business in the 1940s. You couldn't play songs from a film or show until it had had its premiere. Both Bing and Irving had to wait until then before they could imagine the impact "White Christmas" would make.

They soon found out. The day after its first broadcast the record stores reported the biggest rush for a single tune they had ever known. Of course, the studio had seen to it that "White Christmas" was premiered just as the festive season was getting underway. As for Decca, their new disc was the perfect present. It quickly became the top tune on the Hit Parade show and was to do so no fewer than 32 times between then and the show's closure in 1959. That, too, was a record never to be beaten.

Bing Crosby could have retired more than comfortably had "White Christmas" been the only song he ever recorded. Indeed, he could have been a rich man if the half hour spent in the studio making that record was the only work he ever did between leaving school and dying. It's interesting to speculate that, had the song come to him fifteen years earlier, it might well have been just that. Now, however, work as a concept (if not a passion) was important for Bing.

CHAPTER
TWELVE

The Jolson Story

It was the *Kraft Music Hall* that cemented Bing's relationship with his public. To millions, it was the only thing on the radio that they wanted to hear. When Crosby was on the air, young couples stayed home instead of going to the movies. Older people cancelled visits to restaurants. If they went visiting, they made sure they could sit in front of their hosts' radio sets.

This was wartime, so any light entertainment was valuable, but Crosby's effect on national morale is perhaps difficult to appreciate more than half a century later. He only had to sing a song once and the record shops worked out whether it was going to be another big hit or just an also-ran. In truth, there were a lot of those: songs that Bing had been given just before he turned up for his $7,500 stint in the studio and which he didn't care about very much. They were, of course, the staple of his broadcasts, which were prepared, as far as he was concerned, with the same laid-back approach of everything else he did.

His producers took them rather more seriously. Because Bing wasn't around much, they had to pay an even greater attention to detail than normal. No programme was ready to go out less than fifteen minutes before transmission, but then Bing had two great assets: his voice and his ability to sing virtually anything at a moment's notice.

Sometimes, he got it wrong. He either forgot the lyrics of the old songs he had learned by heart or lost the place in the sheets from which he was singing the new ones. That was when it was useful for him to be able to "boo-boo-be-boo".

There was more to the success of the show than that, however. *Kraft* was one of the few radio programmes broadcast without an audience — for a long time he insisted on it and he found that audiences at home liked the fact that other people didn't have any advantage over them, too.

But everything did not go his way. He wanted to record the programmes, but the network wouldn't allow it. They said it would affect the impromptu mood of the *Music Hall*, which people undoubtedly did like.

Throughout the run of his show, he had the services of Carroll Carroll, one of the most talented writers on American radio, a man who always judged the mood perfectly. Bing would have preferred to do no more than just sing on his shows, but the $7,500 required that he did more than that. Carroll knew the way Crosby talked and the results showed. He also knew how his guests talked.

Those guests would prove to be as popular as Bing himself. He had Victor Borge stunning the audience with the first performances of his phonetic pronunciation, giving total new meaning (and new-blown raspberries) to commas, colons and full stops (or periods, as he called them). Bing professed to be enchanted, a rare state of affairs for him.

Other visitors had strong followings, too: James Stewart, Douglas Fairbanks Jnr, Marlene Dietrich and Phil Silvers all came on the show. "We liked to make fun of ourselves and Bing gave us every opportunity," said Fairbanks. "Comedy was very important in those days and Bing's was, on the whole, as much a comedy show as a musical one."

By now, Crosby had a new name that went everywhere with him. He was "The Groaner", an appellation that would be attached to him as frequently as "Ol' Blue Eyes" would be to Sinatra (who was also a guest at the *Hall*, looking so skinny that Bing joked, "He could never stand sideways in class or he'd be marked absent.").

They were worried about each other, Crosby and Sinatra. Bing was afraid that Frankie wanted to take over his throne and nothing the younger man said would disabuse him of that fear. Yes, he would always admit that Crosby had been his idol, but he professed that it was now his turn to be America's number-one singer, especially with all the excitement he had caused at the Paramount Theatre. It was, after all, there that the bobbysoxers had demonstrated that audience reaction was a four-letter word spelt L-O-V-E. They virtually made that love to him in public — swooning and sitting in the theatre from early morning until late at night, with intolerable effects on the theatre's sanitary conditions. They had never done that for Crosby.

But for the time being, at least, Bing's show was the one they all wanted to hear, and to be on. Phil Silvers had his first broadcasting breaks on the *Music Hall*, long before anyone suggested that he don an Army uniform and call himself Ernie Bilko.

Then there was one other entertainer who shook the building to its very foundations — Bing's own first idol, Al Jolson. Jolson came on to the show in the full flush of the success of his biopic, *The Jolson Story*. He was such a sensation on the *Music Hall* that he came back week after week — until people began wondering whose programme it actually was.

Jolson, who had called himself the World's Greatest Entertainer, was never the World's Nicest Person; in fact he had the reputation of walking over fellow entertainers or lesser fry as if they were the pavement on Hollywood Boulevard. He and Crosby had that in common, although Bing had never been known to dismiss a cast in mid-flow and ask his audiences, "Do you want to hear me or hear them?" Jolson did it constantly, because he always knew the answer. On the *Kraft Music Hall*, when Al was a guest, it was always a toss-up as to who they wanted to hear the more, the host or the guest.

With the success of *The Jolson Story*, Bing kidded Al on his new success. He asked him what the badge he was wearing was all about. "It says, AJTWGE — that means, The World's Greatest Entertainer. Bing, did you see my movie?"

"*The Jolson Story*?" queried Bing, who knew the answer perfectly. "Wasn't I a nice guy in that?" Jolson would crow. Bing didn't deny it — or complain. When

Crosby said something that Al plainly liked, Jolson said: "Oh, you're so sweet." People who saw the show that night noted that it was one of the very few times that Bing — the man who hadn't even stopped having dinner with Fred Astaire when he heard that his house had caught fire — showed his emotions and took a seemingly endless time to respond.

On their first programme, they duetted with one of Al's oldest hits, the song he would say was the first he ever sang in public, "Rosie, You Are My Posie". They followed it with "Waitin' For The Robert E. Lee". They were perfect duets, sharing the vocals equally with each other, in one Jolson doing the verse and Crosby the chorus, then reversing it with the number that followed.

Over the next few months, they did a minstrel show with John Charles Thomas and performed the old Stephen Foster numbers "Beautiful Dreamer" and "O! Susanna". On another programme, they were joined by Irving Berlin. Al sang "Lazy" — which most people seemed to think should have been Bing's own signature tune — and the two did a duet of "Alexander's Ragtime Band". That last was one of the great moments of their partnership, with Bing kidding Al on his age — he was over 60 at the time — and Al saying he imagined that the first time Bing heard the 1911 hit was "sitting on your mother's knee, you know, listening to me singing." "No," Bing replied, "I went to the show that day on a go-devil."

That number went down so well that it became their only recorded commercial collaboration — although pirated albums of their radio songs would emerge later.

The discs backed "Alexander" with one of Jolson's first recorded comedy songs, "The Spaniard That Blighted My Life". The tunes were played so often on radio on both sides of the Atlantic that the two were both declared to be "A" sides. They sold more than a million copies. Why they did not repeat the experience no one has ever been able to explain. So the American fans — who had an advantage not shared by those overseas — had to be content with the radio shows. The two would go on to perform "All By Myself", and "Remember", "April Showers" and "The One I Love Belongs To Someone Else", "For Me And My Gal" and a Gershwin medley.

Soon after those shows, Bing treated Kraft and the *Music Hall* the way he threatened to treat Paramount when things weren't going well: he walked out. He cancelled his contract, officially for financial reasons, although there were other issues — mainly that Bing wanted to record his broadcasts and not have to show up every week. They couldn't reach agreement. So Bing packed up and went on to another network. The *Kraft Music Hall*, therefore, needed another host. It turned out to be Al Jolson, who beat Bing to the first place in the radio ratings, something that hadn't happened for a decade.

Crosby had reason to admire Jolson's style. Three years before they teamed up on the *Hall*, Bing had played his first and only real-life role, the biography of the founder of the minstrel show, Dan Emmett, in *Dixie*. (*Dixie* was a lot better than his last screen appearance, when practically everyone working on the Paramount lot was featured in an unfortunate film called *Star-Spangled*

Rhythm. It had provided the first acting chance for eight-year-old Gary Crosby and gave Bing the opportunity to sing his famous anthem "Old Glory".)

It was 1943 and it is not difficult to imagine that, had Jolson not been in the career doldrums at the time, the role might have been his. But it would take *The Jolson Story* to revitalize his professional life. As it was, *Dixie* was not one of Bing's greatest successes.

Jolson himself in those pre-comeback days was busy being one of the first to entertain the troops. Bing followed, although, as we have seen, Hope had got there first. It turned out, however, to be another great Crosby career move.

He went to Europe immediately after D-Day and learned that he was just as popular with the serving men as he was with their wives and sweethearts at home. He was surprised by this. Bing might have had good enough reason not to expect it. He may have had good medical grounds for being excluded from military service, but every entertainer who didn't get his hands dirty in battle was vulnerable to charges of cowardice. In England 25 years before, they would have been sent a white feather.

It was in Britain, though, that Bing had his greatest triumphs. He sang with Glenn Miller. He joked with Bob Hope and performed the latest nonsense song "Mairzy Doats . . ." with him. They appeared with Anne Shelton, Britain's favourite girl singer, who was still in her teens. (She couldn't believe it really was Bing who rang to ask her for tea. She said, "Sorry, I'm seeing the King at Buckingham Palace.")

Bing was guest of honour on the BBC's number-one music hall radio programme, *Variety Bandbox*. Unusually, the show this time was pre-recorded — the BBC knew that it would be played all over the world and were frightened that a live broadcast might be interrupted by the sound of a flying bomb exploding — something that was not calculated to do much for service morale.

It was the time of the blackout, and a ban on more than a dozen people gathering at any one time. When Bing walked to a London restaurant, however, his girl fans took notice, stood outside and shouted for Bing to sing for them. The police advised him that the only way the crowd could be persuaded to disperse would be if the singer did just that. So he opened the restaurant window — once all the lights had been turned off — and sang "Pennies From Heaven" from the first floor of Kettners. Two girls were allowed to play torches on him. When the song was finished, they agreed to go home — and Bing went back to his dinner.

It was no more than the crowd would have expected from such a nice man who had played a priest in *Going My Way*.

CHAPTER
THIRTEEN

Father O'Malley

Bing was not beyond using a few four-letter words —
especially when that bear growled in *Utopia*. "That's not
nice, coming from a priest," said Bob Hope. Thirty years
earlier, back in Spokane, it might not have surprised his
parents if he had decided to take the Cloth. But although
he was extraordinarily influenced by the priests who
were his teachers, that was never likely — the discipline
would have driven him mad.

It is ironic then that in the public imagination in the
1940s, he came to personify the Catholic cleric. That
was what happened when you played a popular role in
those days, and in 1944 there was to be no more
appealing part than that of Father O'Malley in *Going My
Way*. It was the latest incarnation of that Hollywood's
staple — the man in the black suit who was gentle and
kind, but as tough as they came.

The story, about a young New York priest who takes
over a slum church, was originally to be called *The
Padre*. It was written by Frank Butler, the *Road* films
writer, along with Leo McCarey and Frank Cavett.
McCarey, who directed, was a friend of Bing's and had
been the first to suggest that he take the part.

Again, he said no. Like singing "Silent Night", the church was not a subject for levity. "Leo McCarey was an old racetrack and football pal," Bing recalled. "And he always threatened to use me in one of his pictures. After years of joking one day, he finally said he wanted me to play a priest. I told him the church simply wouldn't stand for that kind of casting, but Leo said it would. He sold his idea — and when he finished, there wasn't a dry eye among us.

"Paramount brass thought Leo was all wrong. They couldn't see me in a long, black buttoned-down robe. But Buddy De Sylva, the production head, went along with Leo."

To the public, it was quite a shock. To some, it was an even greater shock that Crosby accepted the invitation.

McCarey would say that, when he began, he only had the characters in mind. There was as yet no story. Bing himself modelled the character of Father O'Malley on a teacher at Gonzaga. Whether that teacher would have sung "Swinging On A Star" is perhaps doubtful, but the song won an Oscar.

More importantly, Bing won one, too — for best actor, beating Cary Grant, Alexander Knox and Barry Fitzgerald, who played the part of the older priest whom Bing came to replace. He was an older, crustier actor, also with Irish roots, who at first resented the younger man and then was charmed by him. Bing did not win the other Academy Award for which he was nominated that year: he was one of the first two men to be up for both the Best Actor and Best Supporting Actor prizes. Supporting Actor was won by Barry Fitzgerald.

It was the first demonstration that Bing Crosby, singer, was also an actor to worry about. Critics were not quite so sure about his achievement. But James Agee would write: "The lessons, if I read them right, are that leisureliness can be excellent, that if you take a genuine delight in character, the universe is open to you and perhaps above all that a movie, like any other genuine work of art, must be made for love."

There were also Academy Awards for best picture, best script, best original story (won by Leo McCarey) and best director (Leo McCarey again).

Bing's Oscar — "this hunk of crockery" — was presented to him by Bob Hope, who would never really stop envying his partner for receiving the recognition that he himself had not achieved. For him, it was Passover again. Bing himself was modest about the win. "It was a war year and all the good talent was away. I figured that they reckoned: 'Give it to the guy, he's not a bad fellow.'"

The not bad fellow was brought back to make a sequel the following year. This time, Father O'Malley's singing was accompanied by *The Bells Of St. Mary's* — a Catholic school where he and Ingrid Bergman, playing Sister Benedict, were rivals to run the roost. It was not at all bad, either, except that it began to look odd to see Bing Crosby in that threadbare sports jacket and the ill-matching socks. The movie was released by RKO/Rainbow, who borrowed Bing for the occasion.

James Agee wrote this time: "The picture is full of shrewd and pleasant flashes. It is also fascinating to watch as a talented, desperate effort to repeat the unrepeatable. But, on the whole, it is an unhappy film."

There were more Oscar nominations: Best Picture for Bing; for Robert Emmet Dolan, who was in charge of the music; for Ingrid Bergman and for Bing's "Aren't You Glad You're You."

Films and records were a vital part of national morale in those final months of the Second World War. The propaganda department of the American Government worked out that they could be used in a different context: Bing could broadcast to Germany, to show them how nice, homespun and peaceful the American people were. His phonetic German earned him an unexpected result — he became incredibly popular among the German troops. They even gave him their own nickname, Der Bingle. It was "Lili Marlene" in reverse. As for the Der Bingle title, it would become part of his persona. For years afterwards, friends and comics on his radio shows would slide the name into their broadcasts. In the 1950s, there was even a record issued under the title.

When the war was over, Crosby found himself singing "I've Got My Captain Working For Me Now" — the post-1918 Irving Berlin tune that was perfectly suited for the mood of returning servicemen. So was *Blue Skies*, the film in which it appeared, which marked the return of the Astaire-Crosby act in yet another assemblage of Berlin tunes — this time mostly standards, like the title song, "How Deep Is The Ocean", "All By Myself" and "A Pretty Girl Is Like A Melody".

There was also the inevitable bespoke tailored number, written specially for this 1946 movie, "A Couple Of Song And Dance Men." Never could two entertainers have had as perfect a "signature tune" for their act, should they ever have needed it. "You Keep Coming Back Like A Song" performed by Bing made its debut in the film, too. It was one of the hits of the year.

"I wish I could have got closer to Bing, though," Fred Astaire was to tell me. Perhaps that's why there really would be no need for that signature tune. They never made another film together.

It was a wonder that Bing found time to work on any movies at all. He was still churning out records every week — at one time the average reached two sides a day — always finding something new to adapt to his own style. There were, as usual, other artists lining up to join him.

When Berlin's stage mega hit, *Annie Get Your Gun*, began its sensational success at about the same time as *Blue Skies* opened, Crosby joined Dick Haymes and the Andrews Sisters to sing the biggest hit from the show: the number that came to be regarded as the national anthem of the theatre, "There's No Business Like Show Business". It was one of dozens of songs in which the Andrews Sisters found Bing the perfect lead. "Is You Is Or Is You Ain't?" was another big hit.

Meanwhile, Bing and Bob Hope were recording all the songs they sang in the *Road* movies. The best was "Put It There, Pal" from *The Road To Utopia*.

Bing's new radio programme, this time on the comparatively new ABC network, was called simply *The Bing Crosby Show* and was aired from San Francisco. Bing thought that a new location would breathe freshness into his old formula, which was why, apart from John Scott Trotter, the personnel on the show changed. To lose Scott Trotter would have been professional suicide and Bing was in no mood to consider ending his business life.

Besides, when the new show began airing, he had already branched out into new professional fields. His own electronics company was in partnership with the Ampex Corporation working on tape recording, which had been developed in Germany but was unknown in America until an Ampex engineer smuggled a couple of machines out of the American zone of the conquered country.

The Crosby show was then not only recorded, as Bing had wanted, it was preserved on tape. Competing network engineers couldn't understand how there was none of the usual needle scratch or surface noise. The electronics development would prove to be one of Crosby's most successful business ventures, until it became obvious that bigger concerns were making more progress than they could possibly achieve. The only failure was Bing's music publishing company. Either there was too much competition already or Bing and the people he employed didn't have the expertise, but it failed to move the industry.

Dixie, on the other hand, failed to move Bing. She was drinking more — at a time when Bing himself was virtually on the wagon — and was growing more and more unhappy at her husband's absences from home and, more than anything, at his attitude to the boys, who at times were positively frightened of their father. Punishment came in more and more severe beatings. No chance of a mere chastisement or a curtailing of allowances. If they did anything wrong, there was a stick to be produced. Even worse was the strap, which as far as they were concerned was as much a part of their father's prop collection and wardrobe as his hat and pipe.

Gary, who was thirteen at this point, would say that the beatings were so painful, "to keep my mind off the hurt, I would conjure up different schemes to get back at him, ways to murder him."

It was quite a beating indeed that they came to expect. "I dropped my pants," Gary remembered, "pulled down my undershorts and bent over. Then he went at it with the belt dotted with metal studs he kept reserved."

Bing actually wrote in 1953: "I don't claim to be any great shakes as a parent. Dixie used to tell me that I was too lax with our four sons. Many a time she's reproached me with, 'You punish them — then ten minutes later you're taking them to a movie'."

That was not how the Crosby sons interpreted their old man's method of discipline. Certainly not Gary. "Quite dispassionately," he said, "without the least display of emotion or loss of self-control, he whacked away until he drew the first drop of blood, and then he stopped."

Bing admitted that he had used the belt, but sparingly. "For instance, when I found that the boys had been into Dixie's room, taken her canary out of his cage and given it what they called 'a summer suit' by plucking its feathers. I 'summer suited' them." He also admitted that his friends thought he was too tough. "I'm particularly known for this at Hayden Lake, Idaho, where we go each August for a month."

The only Crosby son who said he had no complaints was Philip. His elder brother was always a "whining, bitching cry-baby".

Bing had ambitions for the boys. He sent them to agricultural college — because he thought they would make great ranchers, which was probably either a thwarted ambition of his own or a misguided subconscious attempt to prevent their going into show business. Why? Because he didn't want them to be faced with all the heartaches that attached to the theatre or the frustrations of trying to make a movie career for themselves? Or was it simply that he feared the competition they might, at some distant future date, offer him?

Whatever it was, he had them busy during school vacations working at the ranch he had bought at Elko, Nevada, a place with hundreds of head of cattle and where the work was hard, and at times viciously tough. Dixie hated it, possibly because of the way she knew her sons were being treated but could do little about it. They were expected to work from early in the morning until dusk. Their rewards? A meagre allowance of pocket money and the satisfaction that their dad thought reasonably well of them.

But they had to accept the conditions of the other ranch hands and were never allowed to slack. It was the same at the Holmby Hills house, of course. If any of the boys arrived home late — which, when they were 19, was designated as 10.30pm — there would be strong words straight away and the strap before breakfast. Sometimes, he made them live in his garage block, which may have been the least difficult of all the punishments — at least they were away from the old man.

All this was in such stark contrast to the loveable character the fans swooned to in darkened rooms or the one they so devoutly went to see at the movies.

They didn't know about the marital infidelities which were now adding to the various reasons Bing had for staying away from Dixie and their house. His friends realized that his old womanizing had returned, but thought better of doing anything about it. If there was the slightest chance that Dixie didn't know, most of them had come to the decision not to increase her worries.

For Dixie, the disparity between the Bing of the films (and of the public persona) and the Bing she knew at home must have been one of the most hurtful and isolating aspects of the marriage.

The Emperor Waltz had him at his most cuddly: an American gramophone salesman who falls in love with an Austrian countess, played by Joan Fontaine. It was a pretty pointless exercise and Bing looked distinctly uncomfortable wearing Tyrolean costume, but the audiences didn't seem to notice. He was now everybody's big brother and a kindly uncle to the younger ones and that was how they wanted him. Somehow, as long as he had a couple of songs to sing — provided again by the steady team of Burke and Van Heusen — and there was a reasonably pretty girl in attendance, it didn't matter that the scenery looked as though it had been painted by a decorator on an off day.

A Connecticut Yankee At King Arthur's Court (simplified in England at the time of the 1949 release to *A Yank At the Court of King Arthur*) had more to offer: a wonderful comedy trio of Bing, William Bendix and Sir Cedric Hardwicke, singing the now classic "Busy Doing Nothing", which became another big seller in the record shops.

The story wasn't dealt with all that well, but the germ was there — Mark Twain's tale of an American who dreams he is back at the court of the Round Table — and again Crosby's fans cheered the sight of their hero in period costume, despite Bing's own reservations.

He said he fancied being busy doing nothing but couldn't afford to. Not that he didn't have the money. "Assuming I decided to liquidate tomorrow," he said about that time, "I might be worth, I think, about a million and a half dollars in cash." That was a huge amount of money at the end of the 1940s. "I'd like to retire right now. I mean it. But I just can't. It would mean too much disruption and hardship for many people. I've got to keep right on, like it or not."

But it was the *Going My Way* syndrome that seemed to affect everything. The people wanted more of the same. Or perhaps that ought to be corrected — Paramount studios thought that the people out there who bought the tickets wanted more of the same. So, in 1947, *Welcome Stranger* was a feature in which Bing played a young doctor taking over the practice of an older man. Heard that before? Somehow the stethoscope around his neck didn't have quite the impact of the turned-round collar. By the way, the older man was . . . can you guess? . . . Barry Fitzgerald.

Then, after the *Emperor Waltz* and *Connecticut Yankee* films, he and Mr Fitzgerald just happened to get involved in an epic to find the blarney stone. That was *Top O' The Morning*. The film wasn't the top of anything. Nor was *Riding High*, the second film of the same name to be produced by Paramount in seven years — although it did include one classic number, "Sunshine Cake". Crosby's 1950 movie had nothing in common — not even the story — with the earlier vehicle, which was about a burlesque queen. In Bing's film, he was a horse trainer.

He liked racing as much as ever, but golf was still his game. He took part in the British Open Amateur Championship, surrounded by what an onlooker described as "giggling, squirming ladies". Anyone wanting to appoint a man as a film trainer, could, however, still think of Bing Crosby for the job. As we have seen, his films weren't always good. Some were terrible, but people still wanted to see him, wanted to hear him sing, even if there were fewer boo-boo-be-boos, and almost no too-ra-loo-ra-loo-rays.

CHAPTER
FOURTEEN

Anything You Can Do . . .

There were too many indications that Bing Crosby wasn't always the kindest person in the world. His wife and his children could certainly testify to that. Perry Botkin, who a long time earlier had taken over from Eddie Lang (Bing's favourite guitarist who had died following a tonsils operation), decided after being dropped from the Crosby radio show that he ought to set up an organization called PBOBBC — People Brushed Off By Bing Crosby.

Before long, Bob Hope would have reason to sign up for membership. Hope himself had his weaknesses, but on the whole he was well liked by the industry, even those who resented his lack of generosity on occasions. But if Crosby had been honoured by his peers, Bob would be the first to go along to pay him tribute.

When the Friars Club, one of those organizations dedicated to contemplating the entertainment business's navel, decided that the time had come to honour Bob, all the big names turned up to pay him tribute. The place of honour, a seat next to Hope himself, was reserved for Bing Crosby. He didn't bother to turn up to sit in it.

"I never go to those things," he explained afterwards. And, most hurtful of all, "I wasn't hungry."

Later, he was kinder: "My friendship with Bob doesn't depend on appearing at testimonials." Bob Slatzer, who later wrote a book about Crosby and was a publicist on the *Road* films, told me: "Bob was deeply hurt. He would never have failed to turn up for an affair that honoured Bing. There was a great dislike that he developed for Bing after that. I think it was the fact that he might have been a little jealous."

They were indeed jealous of each other, yet Crosby was in the habit of avoiding those things. Many years later, he refused to attend a "do" for British comedian Jimmy Tarbuck. "Who needs a handful of cold canapés and a room full of boring people?" was his explanation. At about the same time, he was introduced to ex-King Constantine of Greece on the golf course. "Hello," he said — and turned his back to get on with his game.

As far as Bob Hope was concerned, Bing's attitude was just another reason to show him that he could better anything that The Groaner could do. It was why when Bing decided to become a baseball tycoon and virtually take over the Pittsburgh Pirates, Bob retaliated with a giant share in the Cleveland Indians. But Crosby was always the baseball boss. Later, he would add the Detroit Tigers and the Los Angeles Rams to his field.

Bing and Bob still took out a lot of their frustrations on the golf course. The Bing Crosby golf tournaments were followed by Bob Hope competitions. There was one thing they both had in common. The players were always all white.

As a result, for the first time — and long before the civil rights movement got going — Bing found himself in the middle of a race row. Joe Louis, the ex-world heavyweight champion, asked him why he never allowed blacks to play in the annual golf event. He did not reply in person. His spokesman told Louis: "Basically the tourney is a gathering of his personal friends and 84 professionals approved by him. It is like giving a dinner party at his home and the table can just accommodate so many."

Hope didn't get a letter like that. He may have wondered why he was left out. Bob and Bing certainly were jealous of each other, although they continued to co-operate in their business and entertainment ventures (which, as we have seen, weren't always one and the same thing).

They also did cameos in each other's movies. Bob wanted Bing for a walk-on appearance in his movie, *My Favourite Brunette*. Bing demanded a fee of $25,000. But there was another side to that story. It later turned out that he sent all the money to Gonzaga University. Cynics pointed out, however, that that meant the money, and much else that went with it, was, therefore, a tax write-off.

Never would a radio season go by without them guesting on each other's shows. "Whenever we announced that Bing would be a guest," Les Brown, Bob's favourite band-leader, told me, "our figures went right up."

They might have gone up across the Iron Curtain too. In 1949, Bing was asked why he didn't go to Prague. A Czech commentator called him, "A greedy American money-seeker who sacrifices art for gold." Bing replied that he would like to go to Czechoslovakia — just as soon as he could buy himself a flak suit.

In 1950, the relationship with Al Jolson had become another one of the central planks of his radio success. Their voices had become complementary: Jolson's was warmer than it used to be and he had become particularly suited to the kind of ballads that Bing had made his trademark. They were now each recording similar numbers, without one having any noticeable adverse effect on the other.

On 24 October, everything was laid on for another of those sure-fire hit shows. A medley of Crosby-Jolson duets dominated the scripts. There were lines about Al's recent return from Korea where he had been the first to go to entertain the troops, and the usual gags about Jolson's age, almost 20 years older than Bing. Their relationship was helped by a unique relationship between John Scott Trotter and Jolson's musical director, Morris Stoloff. "We would share arrangements, so that the music always came out the way their fans wanted and expected it — whoever was playing," Stoloff would tell me.

The day before, Al had travelled to San Francisco. The 24 hours would give him time to settle in and appear at his freshest. But he didn't have that time. The night before the show, he suffered a heart attack and died in his hotel room. In the true spirit of the show having to go on, the *Bing Crosby Show* was broadcast on schedule. Bing's brother Bob (a singer himself, whose own orchestra, the Bobcats, was now a great success) stood in for the much mourned entertainer. But there was no reference to the just-deceased Mr Jolson.

By then, there were new up and coming stars. Frankie Laine, whom Al himself had dubbed "the Al Jolson of 1950", had had a huge success with numbers like "Mule Train" and "Ghost Riders In The Sky". Bing recorded them both, and again his versions sold as though he had been the first to wax them.

Bing's new-record-a-week output was paying huge dividends. This reflected wider trends in American society. The country was experiencing a post-war boom and a large section of "middle America" was becoming more affluent. These new riches had percolated down through the generations and teenagers were spending that wealth — even if it was just pocket money of a dollar or so a week — on records, particularly those new seven-inch 45 rpm platters which were just coming on the market.

For many, the new record-buying habit was focused on one artist: Bing Crosby. His was a situation not unlike that of the Hollywood studios who made enough films to fill the cinemas each week, no matter what the pictures were. His fans would buy the records whatever they sounded like. And now, any song on the hit parade by a competitor, Bing recorded too.

He also began to strike out in a slightly different direction. He let a new face arrange a Crosby song, giving it a feel different from most of the things that

Scott Trotter was producing. "That's How Much I Love You" had a more exciting, more swinging beat. The arranger was Nelson Riddle, still a few years from bringing his talents to Frank Sinatra.

Whenever there was a new Crosby film, the records of the songs in the movie were instantly released, usually in blocks of three or four discs, sometimes more. So a trend was set in motion which would lead eventually to the highly profitable and heavily marketed movie-soundtrack releases of the 1980s and 1980s. *Mr Music* was not particularly significant in this respect.

The film told the story of a songwriter, which gave plenty of opportunities to play new tunes by Burke and Van Heusen. But it was noteworthy in that for the first time Bing played a middle-aged man. The fans noticed it and protested to Paramount, who weren't sure whether to take notice or not. Surely he had grown into that middle age along with his admirers. Could his contemporaries afford to lose him? Wisely, they decided they could not — but would keep the romance.

In *Here Comes The Groom*, there was no doubt about his age — he adopts a war orphan. Frank Capra directed but it didn't have his old mastery. It did, however, have an Academy Award-nominated song. "In The Cool, Cool, Cool Of The Evening" by Hoagy Carmichael and Johnny Mercer, which Bing sang with Jane Wyman, not only jumped to the top of the hit parade, it became a regular on record-request radio programmes on both sides of the Atlantic for years.

All in all, 1951 was a good year for Crosby singles. It was the year when Bing had Louis Armstrong on his radio programme. "Mr Satch and Mr Cros" brought a riotous response as they dwelt on Bing's alleged laziness on his show; the audience wouldn't let them leave the microphone. Everyone was talking about their song — "Gone Fishin'". So much so that Decca made an unprecedented move, another step down that line to the current film soundtrack bonanzas: they bought up the tape from ABC and released it as a single. At this time gramophone records had to be produced in the pristine conditions of a recording studio. Nobody would even dream of releasing a "soundtrack"; any successful songs from a movie, like "In The Cool, Cool, Cool Of The Evening" would always be re-recorded by Decca.

"Gone Fishin'" became one of the best Crosby sellers of all time and can be excluded from no serious compilation of Bing's output. It is funny, rhythmic — and totally believable. Bing and Satch proved to be a winning combination, but although they later made an album together, there would never be another "Gone Fishin'".

There were other big Crosby sellers in that year, although one could not be totally sure that the Crosby who sold the records was Bing. The Groaner decided to record with his son Gary, a gesture seemingly at odds with what we know of their relationship — as was the fact that, most weeks, the 16-year-old Gary was appearing in his father's radio programme. Their versions of the Irving Berlin song, "Play A Simple Melody" (which Bing selected after crossing the Atlantic with Berlin as a fellow passenger), and a new upbeat counter-melody, "Sam's Song", had disc jockeys salivating for months and sold a million or more copies. "Moonlight Bay" also went to the top of the pops.

This was a new, unexpected idea — two Crosbys for the price of one. Gary was getting into the act perfectly. "This is the lad who wound up as my dad," he sang. Bing wasn't going to allow any cheek. "Don't knock that," he warns. "It kept you freeloading for years." But, Gary would insist, freeloading was precisely what he had never done. He had worked hard for every cent his father gave him. And now Bing was ready to play the indulgent father. As he noted in his "conversation" with Louis Armstrong in "Gone Fishin'", he didn't have to work any more: "I've got me a piece of Gary".

Alas for Gary himself, he wasn't totally able to exploit the success into a career of his own. There would be other records but, inevitably, he would always be eclipsed by Bing — although he had a voice not unlike his dad's and people were ready to say that before long he would take over from the old man. Why, he even looked like him: he had hair but the blue eyes could have come from nowhere else. One would have hoped, however, that his home relationship with his father, at least, would have improved. That was difficult when the father persisted in calling the son "Fatso" or "Stupid".

Whatever Bing himself was, stupid he was not. He wouldn't have kept on making movies if he was. But he knew there was money in them. The 1952 film *Just For You* had him playing a songwriter again. It's a film nobody remembers any more, but it did have one song by the veterans Harry Warren and Leo Robin, "Zing A Little Zong", which got an Academy Award nomination.

There was one more movie that year — the last of the conventional *Road* films. The *Road To Bali* was not vintage Crosby-Hope-Lamour. It was the first in colour and the sets were no better than the jokes. It was also obvious that all three stars were not as young as they once were.

Dixie might have noticed the same thing. There were reports of serious rifts in their marriage. She went on a three-month European trip with a couple of friends. Bing went to Britain and France on his own — to play golf. There was a story that he had requested an audience from Pope Pius XII, hoping he would agree to an annulment of the marriage on the grounds of Dixie's constant inebriation, but there is little evidence to back this up.

She tried to patch things up and threw a black-tie surprise party for the birthday of her husband — who hated black ties as much as he disliked pantaloons in film roles. Guests reported that he seemed to show little appreciation of the attention she was trying to shower on him at a time when she herself was beginning to feel desperately ill. She was convinced that she had cirrhosis of the liver. She didn't. She had cancer, but didn't want to admit it or to tell Bing.

She knew that there was more talk of other women in his life, but she told herself it was not true. Forty years later, Bing's behaviour might have been dismissed as a mid-life crisis. They had another word for it at the time, adultery — and it was a word to keep quiet.

Professionally, another thing was also becoming evident, something more acceptable to the fans and a factor that was attracting still more admirers: slowly the Crosby voice was changing. It was becoming deeper and, like Jolson's, warmer. There was an occasional search for breath, the chords were getting shorter, his range was becoming more limited, but in those ballads, there was a maturity that deserved to be appreciated.

Then later in 1952, something very strange happened. Bing made his first dramatic picture, *Little Boy Lost*. Bing was entitled to feel pretty lost himself at the time. Dixie made him go to France to make the movie, but he didn't want to when he realized that she was not well. Not for the first time, his insensitivity had prevented him from noticing the extent of his wife's discomfort.

CHAPTER
FIFTEEN

White Christmas

It was the supreme test and, most people seem to agree, Bing Crosby failed it. Instead of rushing to Dixie's side, he took his time. It has been suggested many times since that it was simply the old Crosby coldness — he didn't really care about other people, not even his alcoholic wife, who over the years had taken on the role of both mother and father — except, of course, when it came to those terrible punishments.

The answer is probably less simple and less harsh. Over the years he had become engrossed in his career. This, together with his introspective nature, led him, selfishly but understandably perhaps, to deny the reality — that his wife was dying. He realized how serious it all was while he was in Europe filming the last scenes in *Little Boy Lost*, ironically not only the story of the boy in question but of a man who crosses the Atlantic only to find his wife dead.

Bing returned home by ship, not plane — possibly a further attempt at escaping reality — and then took the train to Los Angeles. Dixie died a week after his return. It was her 41st birthday.

This is the point when history needs to be revised. Two different accounts have surfaced about Bing's behaviour after his return. One says that he was so distraught that he went into a kind of voluntary purdah, finishing off interior shots at Paramount in a daze. Another description is of a hard superstar who felt free of past responsibilities — at least free enough to start taking an interest in the nubile young women who were round and about. As is frequently the case, the truth was somewhere in between.

The death of Dixie had caught him by surprise, although he knew that she had been ill. He certainly didn't know how he would feel when it happened. He was, by most accounts, devastated. But, to make life bearable for him, he became a more sociable animal than he had been for years. He introduced himself to a 19-year-old bit-part actress on the lot by the name of Olive Grandstaff, which might have sounded all right in Texas where she came from but would not catch the eye of Hollywood casting directors. Soon after her meeting with Bing, she became Kathryn Grant.

While Ms Grant would play a far more significant role in Crosby's later life, at this point it was Mona Freeman, an actress in her twenties also working at Paramount, who was the subject of a number of stories that Bing did his best to hush up. Even if they were true, he was finally coming to terms with his responsibilities to his sons. They were growing up, three out of the four in the last years of their teens. He took them away from their Holmby Hills house and for a time settled down at the Nevada ranch.

He had enough work to keep him busy and did not have to go looking for it. He was still very much on the top of any charts that the show business bible *Variety* chose to print. He was facing competition from the younger performers like Frankie Laine and the constantly weeping Johnnie Ray, but Crosby was still a figure to be reckoned with.

If he was starting to entertain any anxiety that his stardom was waning, this was assuaged by the success of two films which made an impression disproportionate to their quality. *The Country Girl* of early 1954 had Bing teamed with Grace Kelly in the first of their two partnerships. If the film worked, it did so by taking advantage of the moments of melancholy that were beginning to affect him.

He played an alcoholic singer-actor on his uppers who makes a successful comeback thanks to the efforts of his dowdy wife (Kelly) and a thrusting young director played by William Holden. There were a couple of songs, but it was the most dramatic outing of Crosby's career and it won him an Oscar nomination, although not the Award itself — Grace Kelly did get hers.

Bing said he never wanted to play the part in the first place. "I'm a crooner," he protested. But he happily accepted the position of Actor Of The Year, awarded by the American National Board of Review of Motion Pictures.

In subsequent years, it has been customary to look at the film with yellow eyes. Changing tastes have turned a jaundiced gaze on what was in many ways a tour-de-force. Pauline Kael, the eminent critic, was to write: "Rather inexplicably, this sado-masochist morass was one of the biggest hits of the year."

Everyone knew it was a hit. What they didn't know was that Bing had fallen hopelessly in love with Ms Kelly, although she didn't return the compliment. After Crosby's death, his widow sent her a message: "I've been jealous of you because Bing always loved you." She was not joking.

He would tell Kathryn before he married her about the unrequited love affair, although he said that he had been the one to end it. "I struggled to stifle my laughter. Here Bing was apologizing (to Grace) for having chosen me over this regal blonde, the most adored lady in Hollywood."

He sublimated his love in his work. *White Christmas*, later that same year, has also undergone a degree of reassessment in the past four decades. Bing said it was going to be his last movie (although he might just consent to another *Road* film).

It was seen at the time as little more than a rehash of *Holiday Inn*, and when compared with it, came out very poorly. It had a trite enough story, about two vaudevillians who help set up their old army general and turn his failure of a ski lodge hotel into a success. In the intervening years it has become such a staple part of Yuletide TV output that it has gathered around it both a great deal of nostalgia and the undeserved reputation of being a good film. These days, most people who see it are totally won over.

The story was dreadful. Mel Frank and Norman Panama, who wrote the script, told me: "It was a terrible plot that we tried to do our best with after everybody had agreed that the movie they had in the first place would never work."

But story-line apart, the film did have a lot going for it. Crosby was in his best down-in-his-boots voice period and was partnered by Danny Kaye who, although he had none of his old crazy scat singing opportunities, deserved a cheer or two from the Paramount bosses. The fact that he was third choice for the part — of a soldier who saves the life of an officer (who had been a big Broadway star) when a wall fails on him (Panama and Frank were right, the story-line was terrible) — shows just how desperate things were getting. Bing, of course, played the officer.

Fred Astaire had been first in line for the part. After all, this was going to be another one of those films that would be little more than an excuse for Irving Berlin numbers. But he took one look at that script and said, Thanks but no, thanks. Then came Donald O'Connor, who looked forward to renewing the association with Bing which had begun when he was 12, but he had a bad back and had to give it up.

Paramount did what they could to make it work. They filmed it in the new process of VistaVision, their answer to Twentieth Century Fox's CinemaScope. It was another wide-screen process but one which adopted a more acceptable ratio between length and height and had a much clearer picture. The film was also directed by Michael Curtiz, who had a reputation that said he couldn't do anything wrong — until then, that is.

The romantic interest came from Rosemary Clooney, later to work a great deal with Bing, and Vera-Ellen. In one celebrated scene, Bing and Danny were to do a female impersonation number, miming to the Misses Clooney's and Ellen's recording of the song "Sisters". That presented a problem, too. Bing, the man who hated to dress up, resolutely refused to wear women's clothes for the number. The compromise dreamed up by Curtiz, the man who mangled the English language even more than Bing and Danny crucified the dancing, was that the two men would perform with their trouser legs rolled up, a bow in their hair and a huge ostrich fan to their chests.

Strangely, what everyone would have expected to be the highlights of the picture, Bing's two performances of "White Christmas", fell flat. The first was destroyed by a shelling in the army camp where he sang it (to say nothing of Danny Kaye failing to wind up the gramophone at the right moment). The second was submerged in a large production number, complete with little girls and the entire cast. The song would never have been an all-time hit had it depended on this film of the same name, but by then, everybody remembered the way it had been 14 years earlier and, of course, records were again sold by the truckful. Bing's song "Count Your Blessings Instead Of Sheep" won an Academy Award nomination.

It is arguable that the reason the film didn't achieve its expected triumph first time around had nothing to do with the quality of the movie itself (even thought that was a good enough reason). Tastes were now changing. A few months after its release, a young man called Elvis Presley had burst on the scene. Bill Hayley and The Comets were rocking around the clock and the message of that clock was that time was passing by. A new generation was out there buying records that made Bing Crosby sound as though he were part of pre-history.

What made some people wonder was the fact that, unlike other big stars of his generation, he was still making radio programmes. "Television can't kill radio any more than it can kill motion pictures," he said optimistically. "So far as I'm concerned, appearing on TV is the same as being seen in a movie. Too many appearances and the performer is headed for professional disaster. It's impossible for a performer to be at his peak in six or eight movies a year, so you won't find me on TV frequently."

White Christmas was the only movie he made in 1953. "But I did 39 broadcasts and I will do the same in 1954. On the radio I'll talk about the movie, sing some of the songs and maybe josh around a bit with Rosemary Clooney or Danny Kaye or Vera-Ellen." He admitted it was an easy way to make money. "And I don't have to put on a tie, to say nothing of being able to tape the show when and where I like."

It all made him sound positively ancient. The only solution to being cast out among the dodos was to sing the best popular songs by the best possible writers — and try to be part of stories that had a good enough pedigree of their own.

The movie *Anything Goes* seemed to have all that, a remake of the 1936 triumph with Bing in his original role. There was, of course, also the music of Cole Porter and that great title tune. It couldn't go wrong. But it did. It was a lacklustre musical about a transatlantic voyage at a time nobody took transatlantic voyages any more. Even the sets weren't any good. Donald O'Connor finally did get to play with Bing in the film but ought to have regretted it.

The organization that did regret it was Paramount. After twenty-four years and fifty films they and Crosby parted company. The studio system was breaking down under the pressure of competition from television and Paramount, like its competitors, was releasing its contract players from their agreements. That was the official reason, but they also saw the writing on the wall. Making Crosby-type movies was no longer a guarantee of success.

Not that Bing had trouble getting work. In 1956, he was making his first film for MGM since *Going Hollywood*, all those years before. What made *High Society* a film that is still talked about forty years after its release has nothing to do with the story or the direction or most of the acting. It doesn't even have anything to do with Bing's love for Grace Kelly, one of his co-stars. He had taken the hint and behaved coolly towards her — because that was the way he thought she would want it on what was practically the eve of her wedding to Prince Rainier of Monaco.

The film's saving grace, if one can excuse the expression, was that there were some great Cole Porter songs in it. But Crosby was virtually swamped by the rest of the cast. The real excitement was watching Frank Sinatra, Celeste Holm and Louis Armstrong in a clutch of numbers that survived despite the picture, not because of it. Bing had very little to do, apart from singing three or four good songs, including "Little One". He performed "True Love" while apparently squeezing a concertina in a sailing boat with Grace Kelly, who was looking more attractive than she had in *The Country Girl* but seemed to simper rather than act her way through the movie.

The number got an Oscar nomination. It also got her a gold disc. Capitol, who managed to persuade Decca to allow them to feature Bing on their soundtrack discs from the movie, didn't want Grace on the record, but it was difficult to remove part of a duet. Bing was always generous enough to say that she helped make it the song the success it became. The fact that Ms Kelly had become Princess Grace of Monaco certainly did no harm. It made the record into a collector's item — even if there were a million copies of it around.

Johnny Green, then head of music at MGM, conducted the orchestra and made the arrangements seem as perfect as any he had done at a Hollywood Bowl concert. "One of the great experiences of my life," he told me. "If only Bing hadn't been quite so solitary. A conductor needs some kind of rapport with the singer for whom he is preparing the music. Mr Crosby might not have been there."

It should have been a brilliant success as a movie. After all, it was a remake of the 1940 Katharine Hepburn — Cary Grant — James Stewart film. But Charles "Chuck" Walters only succeeded in making it all look static so that it had none of the sparkle, charm or presence of the original, directed by George Cukor.

There were moments when Walters produced what looked like no more than a photographed stage play —

and not a very good one at that. The story concerns an heiress (Kelly) living with her mother in the magnificent mansion in Newport, Rhode Island. Hence it provided a great chance for Louis Armstrong to play at the jazz festival. The heiress has second and third thoughts about marrying for the second time. Bing was her first husband, the one she goes back to at the end of the movie.

Crosby fans were disappointed. His best song was "Now You Has Jazz", accompanied by Satchmo and his band. But the really great numbers featured Sinatra at his very best: the duet with Celeste Holm, "Who Wants To Be A Millionaire", and his number with Bing, "Well, Did You Evah", a clip of which is shown every time someone wants to demonstrate just how brilliant a screen performer Frank Sinatra was. It was clearly Sinatra's number, although Bing did get to deliver a classic line that seemed to sum up his current position. At one point in the song, Sinatra dares to tell Bing, as they get themselves sozzled in the library of the big house, "Don't dig your kind of crooning, chum." To which Bing responds: "You must be one of the newer fellows." It said it all. So did the fact that Bing was not in virtually every frame, as he was used to being.

Yet it made a great deal of money. The album of the songs, showing Bing, Frank and Grace on its sleeve, sold very well — and Bing would say that *High Society* was his favourite film.

Kathryn Grant kept coming and going in his life. They dated occasionally and it was clear that they liked being in each other's company. When she got herself a newspaper column headed "Texas Girl In Hollywood", it was obvious that Bing would be an early subject for an interview — although she would protest that she couldn't remember seeing any of his films and had never collected his records.

She still had acting ambitions of her own and Bing used his influence to get her a contract at Columbia studios. But she wasn't making any great impact in Hollywood.

For Paramount, she had appeared in *Arrowhead*, the Hitchcock classic *Rear Window* and in Bob Hope's *Casanova's Big Night*, and she also played in *Unchained* for Warner Bros. Under her Columbia contract, she had parts in *Phenix City Story*, *The Seventh Voyage Of Sinbad* and *Anatomy Of A Murder*. But luckily she also had academic ambitions and was taking a course at UCLA. Eventually she made up her mind that what she really wanted to be was a nurse.

Three years on and she did indeed qualify as a registered nurse. That would have been the defining event in her life had she not been about to achieve another big ambition. On 24 October 1957, she and Bing were married at St Anne's Church in Las Vegas. Kathryn, brought up as a Baptist, converted to Catholicism in time for the ceremony. He was fifty-four, she was 23, a year younger than her new stepson, Gary.

That there was a wedding at all surprised a lot of people, not least Bing's *other* girlfriend. Bob Slatzer told me, "she thought she was decorating a house in which they were going to live. Bing had proposed marriage to her. Then she had read that Kathryn married Bing and not she." There had, in fact, been three previous dates and venues set for the Crosby/Grant nuptials over the last couple of years but the marriage had always been called off at the last minute and Kathryn's wedding dress put back into storage. These false starts can be attributed to Kathryn's cold feet — a complaint exacerbated by the flood of letters she received, all amounting to the same thing: she was much too young to marry this man, whose fame and reputation would stifle her.

The invitations to the ceremony were no more traditional than they had been for Bing's wedding to Dixie 26 years earlier. With the assurance that Kathryn really was serious now, Bing rang his mother and told her: "We're going to church . . ." Then he phoned the boys.

Now that it had actually happened, Kathryn's job was to remove all remaining traces of the first Mrs Crosby. She no doubt thought that it had to be done, but it wasn't exactly calculated to help relations with Bing's sons, who, as could be expected, resented the idea of another woman in their mother's bed. There would never be a great relationship between the boys and their stepmother, although in public she would extol their virtues, praising their talent. It just never worked out between them.

But Bing was telling everybody that he had never been happier. "It has been a wonderful thing for me. I stay home a lot more. You know, when there isn't a woman around you are always on the go — eat out most of the time and that can get pretty dreary. Since I have got married, I really find it agrees with me."

What he was admitting was that he looked closer to retirement than ever before. "I am just standing by waiting for something attractive. The best thing is to stay away from something you have no feel for. Otherwise you are in trouble. I have managed to give, if I may be immodest, some good entertainment." Nobody could take that away from him.

Nevertheless, for the first time in his life, it was worth asking whether the great Bing Crosby career had finally come to the end of the road.

CHAPTER
SIXTEEN

A Songwriter's Dream

The business was changing and Bing had to adapt to stay with it. Around about the same time that he left Paramount, Bing's exclusive contract with Decca came to an end, too. But he went out with a flourish. The label decided to mark twenty-one years of Crosby recording for them with a deluxe collection of eighty-nine songs, in a package of five LPs called, simply — of course — *Bing*. He linked the songs with a commentary, roughly going through his life. Some of the tracks were the original recordings, like the inevitable "White Christmas", his duets with Bob Hope, Al Jolson, Johnny Mercer and, naturally enough, the Louis Armstrong partnership of "Gone Fishin'". Others, like "Mississippi Mud" were re-recorded with the Buddy Cole Trio. Bing was not about to shatter any illusions and give the impression that he was working hard. Each track, he said, took no more than five minutes to record. Some sounded like it. Others had a freshness they didn't even have when they were new.

Now the man who had made more records than any other human being in history — a record (an unavoidable pun) that still stands — was free to make them for any other company that wanted him.

Now there would be new Crosby records for Capitol, for Pickwick, for Reprise and for a whole swathe of little labels that one might have thought Bing would never have looked at in past years. Ironically, some of his later recordings were among the very best he made.

He got very jazzy on an album released by Verve (and by HMV in Britain) in the late 1950s, called *Bing Sings While Bregman Swings*. The LP, in which he was accompanied by Buddy Bregman and his orchestra, was probably meant to be a Crosby counter to all those Sinatra albums like *Songs For Swingin' Lovers* and *A Swingin' Affair*. It didn't sell very well, but aficionados had good reason to be pleased that he made it. They could hear that warm "new" (or "old" depending how you look at it) Crosby voice singing classics like "They All Laughed", "Have You Met Miss Jones?" and "Cheek To Cheek".

Billy May conducted the orchestra for *Bing And Louis*, a new album for MGM, in which he sang jazz standards ranging from "Way Down Yonder In New Orleans" and "Muskrat Ramble" to "Dardanella" and "At The Jazz Band Ball".

There was a whole string of other albums, usually adopting a theme, like *Songs I Wish I Had Sung The First Time Around*, on which he performed numbers made famous by great entertainers like Al Jolson and Maurice Chevalier. There were also a couple of fairytale records like *Never Be Afraid — A Musical Version Of The Emperor's New Clothes* and *Ali Baba And The 40 Thieves*, with new songs by Sammy Cahn.

127

"It was funny writing songs for Crosby," Sammy Cahn would tell me. "So different from writing them for Sinatra, who was so demanding. Actually, he was a songwriter's dream. He asked me what I was writing for him and he just got on with singing it."

That was Bing's philosophy as far as television was concerned, too. Reluctantly, the man who said he still loved radio so much was by now convinced, like most other big entertainers, it would soon usurp radio as the staple of Americans' leisure time. He hated it. He didn't like the demands of the medium, the fact that, in those days, TV meant live television, that he had to dress up, that everything he had stood for was now being stood on its head.

He had first realized that he didn't like TV when he made his first programme, as the guest on Jack Benny's first special in 1953. He wanted to be casual, but that was always going to be difficult to pull off in a medium that feeds off electricity and adrenaline.

He was partly convinced that he and television were not going to be a perfect match when he starred in a TV version of the Maxwell Anderson play *High Tor*, a 90 minute production that was aired in 1956. He would never stop regretting that he played the part of a newspaper publisher who only wanted to print good news. He sang seven of Arthur Schwartz's specially written songs for the play, which also featured Nancy Olsen and Julie Andrews, at just about the time she was going to wow the world with her Eliza Doolittle in *My Fair Lady*. The picture was made in twelve days, about the time a big-screen movie producer took to decide who was going to provide the coffee and sandwiches.

It would be another 11 years before his own series, *The Bing Crosby Show*, would air. But he didn't fail to accept the value of TV as a medium. Not only did he appear on other people's shows, very reluctantly, but nurtured others' television programmes with his own company. *Ben Casey*, *Slattery's People*, *Breaking Point* and *Hogan's Heroes* owed their existence to Bing Crosby Productions. But no one could say that they were the productions of which he was most proud.

CHAPTER
SEVENTEEN

"Sometimes I'm Happy"

As he himself would willingly admit, Crosby now had a second chance to be a good father. If he admitted it to Gary and his three brothers, they might have been grateful. As it was, the birth of Harry Lillis Jnr in August 1958 only served to increase the tension. It was as though he had eliminated them from any chance of being his true heirs and that was difficult for them to bear.

The births of Mary Frances in September 1959, and of Nathaniel two years later, only made things harder. They knew that Mary Frances, as Bing's only daughter, would inevitably get special treatment, but it was going to be worse than that. Everyone, and not least Bing himself, talked about the Crosby "second family" and although no one said so, it was clear that the chances of there being any diplomatic relations between the two seemed remote.

Man On Fire, the title of Bing's next film, seemed oddly appropriate for his current state of mind. The story, of a middle-aged man divorced by his wife who refused to hand over their son, seemed equally symbolic.

This picture was to be the first with no Crosby songs at all. The title number was going to be sung by the

Ames Brothers. In anticipation of this — and to establish the Crosby connection — Bing recorded the song himself. It was so successful that Sol C. Siegel, the producer of the film, co-starring Inger Stevens, changed his mind and got Bing to sing it over the credits just the same. But it all did nothing for either Bing's reputation or his box office.

The four sons by his first marriage didn't care about that. There was a state of undeclared war, sparked as in so many other wars, by an apparently unconnected event: Lindsay's decision to cancel an arrangement to spend Christmas of 1958 with his father and new stepmother.

Gary had not been well and Lindsay decided instead to spend the holidays with his elder brother. Kathryn was incensed. So was Bing, who hated the idea of his wife being snubbed in this way. They didn't just row over this, they took action in a way that was so determined that it became the *casus belli* for a feud that never totally resolved itself. They sent back all his Christmas presents.

Gary would say that it was the cause of a "bitter estrangement" between him and his brothers and their father. "Dad did something last Christmas that I felt was far from right." He told a writer that he was still smarting about "all that propaganda pop about us wanting to be ranchers".

There were other reasons for things not being the way they ought to have been between father and talented son — like Bing paying for a cleaning woman to look after Gary's apartment, but with instructions to spy on him and report back to The Groaner.

Bing himself was not unaware of the way that his "first family" looked towards him. Nor did he deny his responsibility in the situation. "I think I failed them," he was to tell Hollywood Associated Press writer Joe Hyams, "by giving them too much work and discipline, too much money and too little time and attention. But I did my best and so did their mother."

Yes, he said, there were times when he got "out of patience" with them. "But the jury isn't in yet on what kind of citizens my boys will make". The jury would come back before long with verdicts that they were citizens with a great many problems — many of them due to their relationship with their father.

When Gary was called up for army service — he had his own CBS contract and was in Australia with Louis Armstrong when the papers came — he was drinking himself to oblivion, sometimes four bottles of brandy a day, frequently combining the booze with a dosage of diet pills. He ended up in a psychiatric ward. But he would say that the tough army discipline was "nothing compared with what I had to endure at home".

He made a handful of films, but he continued to suffer from mental illness. He would break down and cry for his mother, who he insisted had, in fact, killed herself. Yet over a bottle, he would say that he loved his father, even though Bing hated him.

There would be constant drunken escapades involving the other boys, court appearances for drunken driving, fights between them at nightclubs. But in a family spirit the four formed their own act and starred at the Sahara Hotel in Las Vegas. Much to their surprise, Bing and

Kathryn came to the show. Typically, their father didn't tell them he was coming or call round at their dressing room afterwards. But he made nice comments about them to the press, saying how pleased he was about their trying to "get ahead without the old man's money".

The Crosby Boys, as they called themselves, might have looked a sure-fire winner, but they were the possessors of diverse personalities and none of them could be sure of the reliability of the others.

After a painfully short existence, they packed in their act and Gary went it alone. He was given a lot of help by his father's friends, particularly since so many pressmen were calling him "the new Bing Crosby". To say no, the stars figured, would be to say no to Bing and he was much too important in show business for them to risk doing that. Gary made an album with Sammy Davis and toured again with Louis Armstrong as well as with Bob Hope's accompanists, the Les Brown Band. He sang with a group who sounded very much like the Andrews Sisters — another attempt to make the connection between the two generations of Crosbys.

But his drinking got the better of him. One night at the Tradewinds nightclub in Chicago, he was so inebriated that he had to be dragged off the stage. A statement was issued that he had a bad throat — a further echo of his father's early life — but it was the end of his own life as an entertainer. It did persuade him, however, to go "on the wagon", a step of which his father totally approved. (He was to be left more money than any of the other brothers in his father's will, on the grounds that he was the one who had done the most to rehabilitate himself, but, as we shall see, that would not be the end of the story.)

Bing would learn a lesson or two from the way he behaved with the four sons given him by Dixie. His new family were treated very differently — at least by him. He would say that he left the disciplining of his three youngest children to their mother — who was quite adept herself at wielding a battered old hairbrush. In fact, he protested that she was too strict, which must go down as one of the greatest of all ironies in this story.

As part of the decision to make a new life with the new people in his life, Bing took Kathryn and the kids to a new house in the village of Hillsborough outside San Francisco. He would say that he was at home there as he had never been at home anywhere outside of Spokane. But, even so, Kathryn would complain that he was not there enough. He was spending more time playing golf — "a kind of desultory past-time", as Crosby, having browsed through his Thesaurus, would put it — if he wasn't hunting in Spain or Scotland, or at home. He even became one of the founders of Ducks Unlimited — a project through which he and other hunters raised enough money to buy four and a half million acres of habitat for waterfowl. And there was also fishing in Canada or Mexico, which he loved, unlike Bob Hope, who would always say that he couldn't understand the enthusiasm for it: "Fish don't applaud," was his philosophy.

Kathryn didn't complain. As she said: "Bing needs a buddy, not a sweetheart." It was a situation of which she had been given due warning. When they were engaged, the occasion was marked not with a diamond ring from her fiancé, but with a saddle.

She was still anxious to be taken seriously as an actress. For ten years, once the children were secure away in school, she would go on tour, playing in a succession of plays, including both *Pygmalion* and its musical version, *My Fair Lady*.

Bing was growing conscious of the advancing years, even though he was still in his late 50s at the time that Kathryn was out on the boards herself and he was contemplating his next film. There were still a few of them to come, like a promotional picture made for the *Saturday Evening Post* called *Showdown At Ulcer Gulch*, "an adult Eastern" in which he and other veterans like Hope and Groucho and Chico Marx took part.

Later, in 1959, a new commercial movie, *Say One For Me*, could have come and gone without anyone knowing. The only interest was the fact that, for a third time, Bing was playing a priest, this time trying to save a showgirl, played by Debbie Reynolds, from a fate worse than appearing in the movie. It had none of the charm of either *Going My Way* or *The Bells Of St. Mary's*. The only funny incident on stage was when he tripped over his cassock. "I forgot you have to hitch these things up," said the man who for a few weeks was called Father Conroy. It proved he knew what he was doing when he said he didn't like putting on costume.

High Time — his 1960 film about a widower going back to school and falling for the delectable Nicole Maurey — deserves to be better remembered than it is, if only because it featured "The Second Time Around", one of the best of the last batch of Crosby songs and one which was clearly resonant for him. Despite all the cynicism about the comparisons (almost the competition) between Kathryn and her predecessor, it really did seem that, to Bing, love was better the second time around. Mrs Crosby said it was "a very special song for me".

Not quite so good was the second time around for the *Road* films. *The Road To Hong Kong* was one of the big movies of the 1962 season, but it was fraught with problems, foremost of which was a general lack of merit. It had glamour, it had colour, it even had spaceships. But it didn't have Dorothy Lamour in anything but a cameo and, most important, it didn't have the panache of the old Paramount series. The film, made by United Artists in England, had all the marks of an attempt to cash in on past triumphs with none of the know-how. Even the unexpected cameos for Frank Sinatra and Dean Martin could not make it look like it had gone through any serious budget considerations.

The spaceship seemed to be made with tin foil — which it probably was. Even Bob Hope's gags appeared to have been written by a second division joke factory. But Bob and Bing clowned it up like . . . like what? Like a couple of old timers who had once been brilliant and were now doing performances for those who remembered them at a retirement home.

As far as the two principal stars were concerned, it might best be recalled for a serious row. Hope wanted and expected Dorothy Lamour to have her usual part. Bing didn't mind whether she did or didn't. When

United Artists announced from on high that she was now too old to play the vamp of old, he said, "Fine", and got round to suggesting alternatives — like Brigitte Bardot or Gina Lollobrigida. He couldn't see the logic in Hope's argument that it would be less outlandish for a couple of superannuated performers like them to have a woman of their own generation. Bing insisted that it was glamour that sold films.

Eventually, the studio came up with the idea of a British girl star for a picture made in a British studio. Joan Collins hit the jackpot and looked sexy in an early-1960s way.

Neither Bing nor Bob was unhappy about working in Britain, a country where they had played golf as successfully as anywhere else — sufficiently a recommendation to convert them to the idea. They not only worked together in the same studio, they lived in the same house, a stately home called Cranbourne Court at Winkfield, in the heart of the Berkshire countryside. It was close enough to the studio to make the daily journey convenient — and near enough to Sunningdale golf course to swing the deal that they would share the $400-a-week rent. (Money was always important. And his public knew it. When Bing went to Ireland, a wag shouted from the audience, "Can't hear you Crosby, stand on your wallet!")

There were few problems once the movie went on to the floor — except something which had never happened before in the entire Crosby career: he recorded "Let's Not Be Sensible" but, for reasons no one could adequately explain, the last word of the song, "love", was mangled on tape. It was spotted after the filming was completed and Bing was asked to re-record it. He refused: he was a star, not a pick-up artist. So Michael Holliday, a Crosby sound-alike, was brought in to finish the line for him. It would take a very serious Crosby aficionado to spot the difference.

The film — which featured what should have been taken up as the Bing-Bob signature tune, "Team Work" — was to be the last of the series. It was, to say the least, a pity that the monumental *Road* pictures couldn't go out on a higher note. The fortunate thing is that nobody now thinks of *Hong Kong* when reviewing the place the original *Road* films held (and hold) in the affections of a huge audience over an equally huge part of the world. *Road To Singapore* and *Road To Morocco* needed no gratuitous additions to their roster to make them seem important.

Bing himself wasn't that thrilled with it. He thought he was over the hill and gave himself no more than another five or six years to keep on singing.

Over the next few years, there would be talk of more pictures in the series: *Roads* to the Moon and Bombay were both touted. In 1977, Melville Shavelson more or less sold them on the notion of a *Road To The Fountain Of Youth*, but, as will become clear, Bing would not be available to make it.

By now, he was more or less the elder statesman of the world in which he had for so long been king. He didn't aim to compete with rock 'n' roll — he didn't even try to understand it, even though in "Now You Has Jazz" he had referred to "everyone singing, everyone swingin' that rock, rock, rock 'n' roll".

There was another confession he had to make to himself: that in his own genre another king had come along and planted himself firmly on what had been Bing's own throne for what would turn out to be another thirty years. Frank Sinatra sang the old songs, but with a verve that Bing couldn't match. Crosby knew when he was beaten and accepted it. If there were still enough people out there to buy what songs he did record or to go to see the films he still wanted to make, that would have to be enough.

He was ready to bend the knee to the new monarch, whom he respected and called a friend. But the friendship at this time was on a precarious footing. Mr Sinatra was not a man to trifle with. A mere askance look was enough to end a relationship of years.

The threat came via the White House. President John F. Kennedy had been Sinatra's idol for years — Frank had produced and presented the President's inauguration concert. Many say Sinatra was responsible for JFK's hair's-breadth election victory in 1961 by introducing him to the Mafia, who secured the labour union vote. Now, however, Kennedy was beginning to distance himself from the blue-eyed crooner. He was taking the advice that a continued association with organized crime could cost him the next election.

Kennedy had previously accepted a Sinatra invitation to stay at his house when he was in the Los Angeles area. Everything had been laid on, a suite of rooms, even his hotline telephone. Then, a couple of days before the visit, it was announced that the President wouldn't be coming after all. He would stay with Bing Crosby. Sinatra was devastated. His relationship with Camelot was destroyed. But, surprisingly and admirably, he bore no grudges against Bing. Perhaps the old adoration for the man in the sailor's cap was too strong to die.

In 1964, the year after the Kennedy assassination, Bing and Frank cemented their relationship. He played a phoney preacher in a Sinatra "Rat Pack" spoof on the old gangster era movies, *Robin And The Seven Hoods* — a good concept that, to work, needed the delicacy of a fine silver spoon, but which, in the event, was handled with a heavy spade.

It was a picture that was set for trouble from the word go. Gene Kelly was its first director, but he bowed out when he realized that his own ideas of professionalism were not shared by Sinatra, Sammy Davis and Dean Martin, who saw it all as a good chance to have a great time. Bing, for once not playing the loner, seems to have been flattered to be included in the fun and certainly wasn't fazed by the lackadaisical attitude of his fellow actors towards rehearsal and multiple takes.

It all showed. Bing's song "Mr Booze" was a laugh, but the big number was Sinatra's "My Kind Of Town" and Crosby didn't really get a look in. Saul Chaplin, Gene Kelly's deputy, who also resigned when he saw the way things were going, told me: "I couldn't stand the lack of responsibility all the stars — Bing included — seemed to display. It was a shock to the system."

By then Bing was finally making a TV series. *The Bing Crosby Show* was aired for the first time in the autumn of 1964. The format was based on a family — not unlike the hugely successful Bill Cosby shows of 20 years later. Bing played the father of a gang of teenagers. Gary and his brothers must have winced at the irony. Bing himself saw the irony in working so hard on a weekly programme. After twenty-two weeks, the half-hour series came to an end and nobody was too upset. The ratings, which started out good, seemed to tie up with Bing's own feelings.

But there would still be other Crosby TV appearances. Once a month, between 1968 and 1970, he was the presenter of *Hollywood Palace*, sharing the role with George Burns, Martha Raye and Judy Garland. And there was another tradition in the making: in 1966 came the first *Bing Crosby Christmas Eve Special*. Naturally, he always sang "White Christmas". Kathryn was on screen with him and, as they got older, his second family, too, but never the first. It was another cause for friction between the two Crosby camps.

The older boys could only smile ruefully when they heard that their father would wait for his two new sons as they left school — and try to persuade them to play golf with him. Nathaniel accepted more readily than Harry and at the age of 16 had a handicap of five (at school, his handicap was coping with lessons).

Cinema fans had their own cause for unrest. Bing had been unable to sign for the part MGM wanted for him, the lead in *How The West Was Won*. So instead he chose to commit an act of sacrilege. He was the star of a remake of one of the finest Westerns ever produced, indeed one of the best of all Hollywood films. Playing in the new version of *Stagecoach* would not have been a good idea at any time. But he said: "It was a chance to do character and I wanted to do it."

The fact that this would prove to be Bing's farewell to the film business made it all the more poignant. He would not make another picture on his own account, although he would narrate a couple of travelogues and make a cameo appearance in Bob Hope's own last film, *Cancel My Reservation*. Musically also he was winding down: he made an album with Count Basie, but he admitted that "there isn't much call for records of mine any more".

Hence a career which had been launched with panache and a pioneering thrill petered out in a rather undistinguished fashion. The fans who would have wanted to stand and cheer simply disappeared out of cinemas, not even given the chance to put a handkerchief to their eyes.

He himself would say there was no chance of his doing the kind of movies that were filling the theatres. "How the hell are you going to raise children to be good citizens if they have to be exposed to things like these?" he asked and there were many who shared his sentiments. Fred Astaire told me, for instance: "They're showing films you could be arrested for seeing in your own home."

Bing added: "They see actors and actresses whom they adore involved in the seamiest capers and they feel it's the sophisticated or chic way to behave. They see marriage and the family debased and derided and every licence glorified . . . They are selling, furiously, moral irresponsibility. I think it's wicked." Rather rich, one might feel, coming from one whose own youthful capers were far from pure. But Crosby probably felt that it just wasn't the sort of material that was fit for movie entertainment.

Bing, though, was possibly trying to make up for lost time. He set about enjoying himself. Because there was less hard work now, there was more time for playing with those buddies, at least the few who genuinely felt they could get close to him. As he sang in one of the last songs he recorded: "I refuse to grow old, I can be young till I die." All he wanted, the lyric said, and the only thing for which he would trade his seventy years was "seventy more".

By then, he had seen things happening that he didn't like. In 1966, his brother Everett died. It gave him a sense of mortality. That was natural for any man of his age in any position, but he began to see dangers where he had previously not bothered. When, in the early 1970s, his neighbours at Hillsborough, the William Randolph Hearsts, had to deal with the kidnapping of their daughter Patty, Bing worried that it could happen to him and his. He built a high wall around his property and brought in security guards. He hung a megaphone over the tall iron gates so that visitors could announce themselves. In 1973, after the Christmas holidays, which were always the high spot of his year, he checked himself into hospital feeling ill. He was very weak and had been suffering chest pains while on an African safari. The doctors diagnosed a golf ball-sized abscess. Bing was momentarily relieved. He was scared of cancer. The doctors probed more — and discovered that the abscess was indeed attached to a tumour. An operation was performed and about a third of the lung was removed.

Bing had two fears: that it could prove fatal and that it would mean that his voice was in peril. As it turned out, neither was on the immediate agenda. After a rest of three or four months, the doctors announced their conclusion that they could see no evidence of any more cancer. As for his voice, it was virtually unchanged. He went to London to make a few records and the now very deep Crosby tones still had the old lilt about them, even though it was clear that he couldn't hold a note for as long as he once did. His breathing was not the aid to that instrument of his that it had once been. But there was a charm in the new warmth he presented on the newly pressed vinyl discs and the cassette tapes which had started to rival them.

His reputation as a hard man was sublimated for the public. Indeed, he could be very pleasant. About this time, I was writing my biography of Irving Berlin and asked Bing for an interview. He consented instantly. An appointment was made to meet at his hotel. As luck would have it, my train broke down and I arrived twenty minutes late. I found him waiting on the hotel doorstep, pipe in mouth and he said it didn't matter, let's go inside and talk.

With the work that he did, he was conscious of wanting to make an impact now. He knew that, in his seventies, his future was limited, a fact only emphasized by the death of his brother Ted in 1974, followed the year later by Larry.

It had been a full life, to say the least. He had done everything but star in a Broadway show, but it was too late for that now and he would never have enjoyed the pressure of seven performances a week. But there was a yearning somehow to go back to his earliest days, the ones with Whiteman and before. He floated the idea of a stage act — and managements all over America showed their excitement.

Bing Crosby And Friends had Bing singing his old numbers on stage, accompanied by Kathryn, Rosemary Clooney and the Joe Bushkin Combo. The first show in 1975 was so immensely successful that more performances were booked from coast to coast. Then he took the show to London. It was a sell out at the Palladium. It was the best thing he had done for years. Significantly, he enjoyed it more than anything he had done for years, too. "Sometimes I'm Happy" was the double edged message he would sing to Kathryn. But Ted Rogers, chosen by Bing himself to be his comedy partner, certainly found him a happier warmer individual than earlier stories had suggested. In London at the time Bing made an LP with Fred Astaire, two elderly gentlemen singing songs of their youth. Bing's Palladium audiences were said to be mainly middle-aged and elderly, but there was evidence that he had found a new public, too. They were the people who said they wanted to see more of him on TV.

The opportunity for this came early in 1977 when, before 1,200 people, he starred in a CBS special to commemorate an event that was as important to show business as it was to Bing himself — his 50th anniversary as an entertainer. He was enjoying himself immensely. He liked the show. He liked the songs he had to sing. He liked the people with whom he was playing. At the end, it was time to say thank you to all those folks who had helped it go down so well. He turned round to bow to them, took a couple of steps back — and fell into the orchestra pit.

He was rushed to hospital, from which came the usual crop of rumours — he had broken his back, he was seriously ill, he was dying. None of that was true. He had ruptured a disc in his back, but it was not considered life threatening. Indeed, he went back to playing golf without his game appearing to have suffered very much.

He was well enough in September 1977 to go back to the London Palladium with his *Friends* show. Before he went on stage, he was in a studio recording a new album. I met him that day. He was feeling pleased with himself. Four new numbers had been put on tape in two hours. "In the old days, we used to record three numbers in four hours. Today, the equipment is so much better and I think the musicians are, too."

But he wasn't easy to work with. The producer called for a second take. "Why?" Bing asked. "I think we can do better," said the man. "I don't," said Bing and insisted that they move on to the next number.

The new album was called *Seasons* and included a tune for each part of the year, from "June In January" and "April Showers" to "September Song" and "Sleigh Ride". He was feeling so good that when I dared ask about films, he said: "If the right part comes along; one I could handle and with good people, good actors, good names. I'm always asked to do cameo roles, you know, like Fred Astaire has, but I haven't liked the films." He was about to get back on to his old hobby horse. "They always seem to strike me as a bit dirty." He didn't like the "salacious" movies of the day now any more than he had last time he was asked.

This time in the Palladium show, Bing was joined again by Ted Rogers and Kathryn but also by Mary Frances, Harry Lillis Jnr and Nathaniel, who were reprising their parts in the *Christmas Eve Special* they had just filmed at the ATV studios at Elstree. They loved the experience, although they would admit that their presence only lent additional evidence, as if it were needed, of just how good their dad still was. He outshone them all.

They might have appreciated the fact that other people thought he was a little too casual about the way he practised his leisure activities. He was banned from Claridges hotel for practising golf strokes in the corridor. Years before, he had been arrested in Paris for sleeping on the grass near the Champs Elysées. Now, though, he was anxious to impress on them the dignity of the family.

But if the show gave the impression of a happy family, it was a deception. There was talk among close friends of a divorce. Kathryn was fed up with his chauvinist outlook on life. As she confessed: "He was a pretty cute kid when it came to convincing a girl that what she really wanted was to stay at home and scrub floors." She was fed up with the way he would interrupt any comment she made while watching sport on television. "What the hell do you know?" he would snap.

But none of this was obvious at the Palladium. At the end of the last show on 10 October, Bing called out to the audience, "I love you" and clasped his arms around him, as though taking into his embrace everyone sitting in the stalls and the balconies. Rosemary Clooney was to say: "Bing had never been that demonstrative to an audience in his life." Kathryn might have said that he had never been that demonstrative to her either. She always said that he could never say those words.

And then he went on to do a broadcast at the BBC's Maida Vale studios. He was getting to like Britain more and more. He had good reason to believe that he was appreciated more in England than he was anywhere else. At the end of the 1970s, he certainly wasn't being given evidence of that kind of appreciation at home in the States — or was it, after all those years, just love?

If it was, he found difficulty in understanding what the fuss was all about, especially when, if he thought about it, he hadn't had a hit in twenty years. "I am not a great actor and I am never going to create anything of lasting importance. So, no matter what I have done . . . there is little promise of great artistic satisfaction in it. With the exception of a record or two, I don't think I have ever done anything really worthwhile . . . Every man who sees one of my movies or who listens to my records or who hears me on the radio believes firmly that he sings as well as I do, especially when he's in the shower." And he admitted that he might have done better. "I often wish

I'd been more zealous in my life, but laziness seemed to keep getting in the way."

Only his golf could rival the kick he was getting now at the age of 74. But he admitted, "I am basically a lazy man. I do a little scratching. And a little bending." There was an invitation to go to Spain to play golf, an invitation that he couldn't possibly turn down. Certainly, Kathryn wanted him to go, although people said they weren't sure whether that was simply to have him out of the way.

It was a Friday morning that he went on to the greens of La Moralejo Golf Club near Madrid, feeling relaxed and very contented at what he had done in England. Maybe he was also thinking of his contentment at what he had been doing for 50 years. After all, he had gone a very long way without giving much evidence of having worked terribly hard at doing it.

This was the life and he was going to enjoy it to the full. It was a good game and his score was impressive as he got to the 17th hole. He and his partner were in the lead against the professional Valentin Barrios and the club president. His ball, to quote one of his songs, "went straight down the middle" and landed in the hole. He looked, waved his putter — and fell. His partner, another Spanish golf pro Manuel Pinto, assumed he had slipped on the damp turf and ran to help him get up. Except that he couldn't get up.

Bing had had a massive heart attack. On the way to the Red Cross Hospital in Madrid that heart stopped beating and there was nothing any of the paramedics could do to revive him.

The crooner they called The Groaner was dead. What he himself in one of his very last songs, said was "the crazy misadventure called life" was over. The song had ended.

CHAPTER
EIGHTEEN

A Crazy Misadventure
Called Life

President Jimmy Carter issued a statement praising a great American. It came just minutes after the US Ambassador to Spain phoned Kathryn to tell her the news — which showed just what a great American he was considered to be. Kathryn told her children, but by most accounts his four older boys heard about their father's death on the radio, a fact not guaranteed to improve their relationship with the other Crosbys.

Bob Hope cancelled his TV Show. It is legitimate to wonder if Bing would have done the same had the positions been reversed (as we have seen, he said nothing after the death of Al Jolson).

Almost everyone else who heard it thought that Bing's death was a personal loss, which accounted for the 3,000 people who packed into New York's St Patrick's Cathedral for a special mass. Services were held all over America, especially at his local church, Our Lady of Angels at Hillsborough. But the actual funeral service was at St Paul's Church at Westwood in Los Angeles. The interment was at Holy Cross Cemetery, close to where Dixie was buried and where his parents had been laid to rest. Bing made provision for a possible wish that Kathryn might make in the future: the grave was eight feet deep, enough to allow her to be buried on top of his coffin if she so desired.

He also gave her an income of about $300,000 a year — but it was his lawyer who would administer the estate. Kathryn was reported to be furious. She was said to be "depressed and feeling horribly betrayed". But, as in all the best Hollywood stories, she would later deny that her husband was anything but "the most beloved man I ever met".

Only Gary was mentioned for an immediate bequest. The others were deliberately told that they could have a share of his multi-million fortune, but at dates far into the future and no other claims could be entertained.

Celebrities all over expressed their grief. To Frank Sinatra, "He was the father of my career, the idol of my youth, a dear friend in my maturity." Bob Hope said he was "overwhelmingly shocked".

His younger children simply grieved at his absence. They wept. He had made a good life for them and they were in the early stages of careers that they knew met his approval. Harry was studying theatre at the London Academy of Music and Dramatic Art. Mary, who would go on to shoot JR in *Dallas*, seemed on the threshold of a great acting career. But at the age of 38, she was complaining that she couldn't get work. "It's been a long time since I was flavour of the month", so she hoped she could become a film producer. All she needed was the money.

Nathaniel was on the way to being a highly proficient golfer.

Nobody could be totally sure that the older boys would ever be equal causes of pride. But few would have imagined the great tragedy that befell them. Both Dennis and Lindsay, their confidence and personalities fatally crushed by their father's taunts, shot themselves dead, within the space of a few years. The tragedies went on. Gary, the one son who Bing thought had something — perhaps because he looked so much like him — wrote a book that seemed to outdo even Joan Crawford's daughter's *Mommy Dearest*. *Going My Own Way* detailed the authoritarian behaviour of his father and served as a receptacle for all his anxieties, frustrations, resentments and hatred. He said at the time that Philip — the brother who had called him a "whining, bitching cry-baby" — was "as far as I am concerned, dead". But Philip would be the only brother ever allowed to come to terms with life. In August 1995, Gary, too, died.

Perhaps the most interesting questions are the most difficult to answer. What, for instance, was so special about Bing Crosby that made him so beloved by his audience and so resented by those near to him?

Of course, he was a complex man — a more straightforward sort wouldn't have had those problems. But you can't, unlike so many other vital show business characters, say that he lived only for his work. If he did, it was a very closely guarded secret. He called his autobiography, written almost half a century ago, *Call Me Lucky*. He was very lucky indeed. Lucky to be blessed with a talent he would have been the first to admit was God-given. Lucky to have used that talent so wisely. Lucky to have achieved so much. But unlucky to have been unable to love so many people who wanted to love him.

The luck that he did have gave him a star quality which is still undefinable. But you knew it when you heard it and you knew it when you heard Bing Crosby. Those who have it can survive almost anything.

It was, as he sang, what life was all about.